Fly-Fishing Gui[de] To The Olympic Peninsula

Price Lake

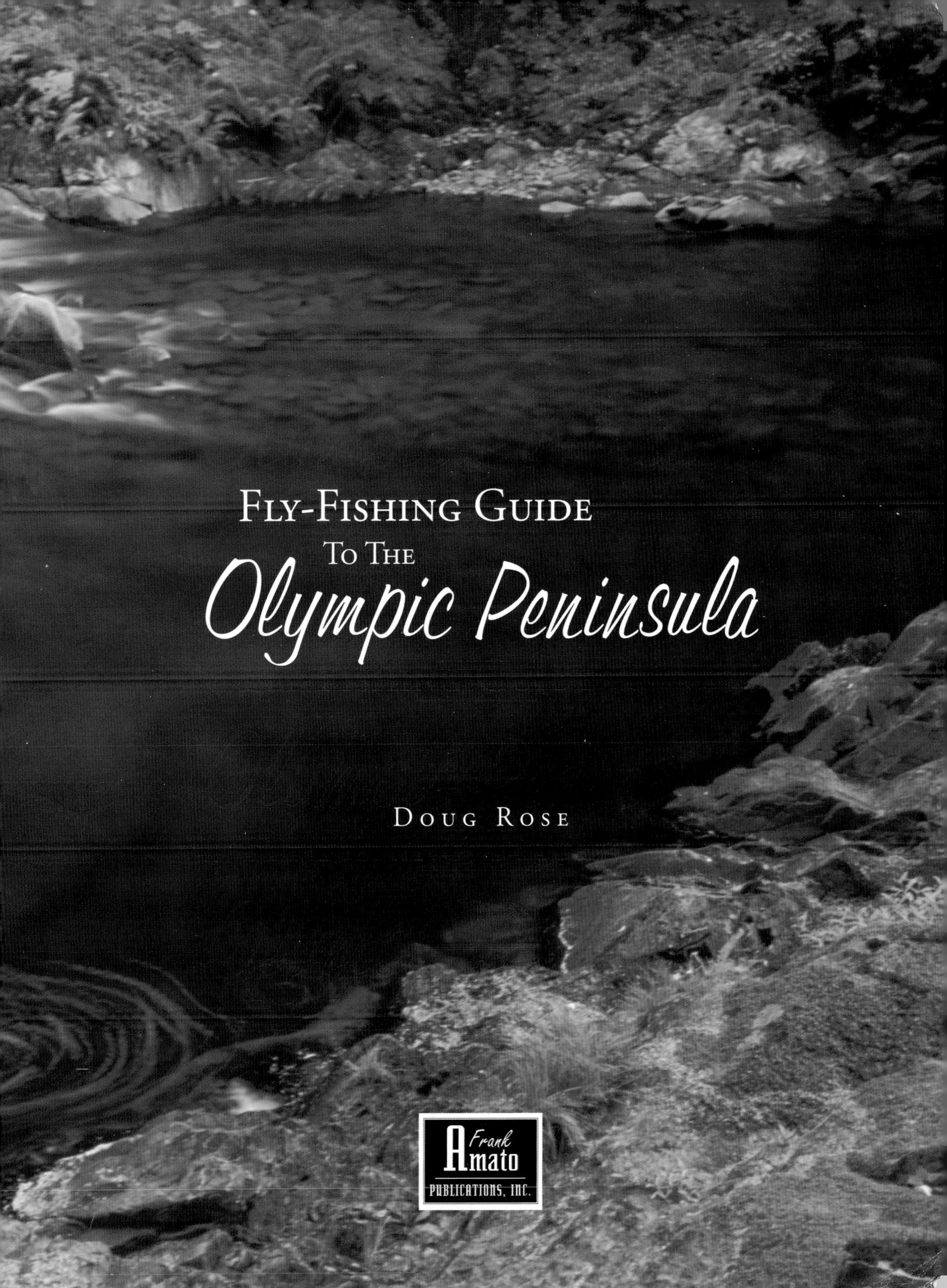

Fly-Fishing Guide To The *Olympic Peninsula*

Doug Rose

Frank Amato Publications, Inc.

This book is for Eliana, as always.

"Salmon and steelhead run these streams in the Fall and Winter, cutthroat trout in the Summer. The Quinault Indians use canoes, hewn by hand out of cedar logs. Memories of my hours with them on fast waters, fishing for cutthroat, are bright. There are pools where one can hold a canoe for several casts with a fly. But in most places the water of the Quinault is too swift for that. One cast at the point of a log, one on the edge of white water below a swirl, one in an opening left by vine maple that partially covers flat water, one where a graceful red alder touches a pool. One cast, a wait of a split second while the fly drifts and the canoe shoots on. Almost before the fly can be retrieved the canoe is above another spot. The timing must be perfect, the cast must bring the fly down softly, the reprieve must be quick. This is exquisite fishing."

William O. Douglas
Supreme Court Justice
"Olympic Mountains" from *My Wilderness*

Acknowledgements

I could not have written this book without the assistance of many people. First and foremost, Dick Wentworth showed incredible generosity, warmth and patience, and I've come to think of him as a friend. I am also deeply indebted to Don Kaas, Dave Steinbaugh, Les Johnson, Ron Hirschi, John McMillan, Dick Goin, Rick Endicott, J.D. Love, Joe Uhlman, Joe Aldrich, and Jeffrey Delia for their anecdotes, observations and flies. John Alevras, Curtis Reed, George Binney and Bob Triggs contributed productive and beautiful Olympic Peninsula fly dressings. Olympic National Park's fisheries biologist Sam Brenkman offered valuable advice and information of fish in the park, and British Columbia's Van Egan and Art Lingren were very helpful with information on Haig-Brown's fishing trips to the peninsula. As in my last book, John McMillan contributed many wonderful photographs, as did Joe Uhlman, Jeffrey Delia. Olympic National Park, and the Washington State Historical Society. Bill McMillan, as always, offered wise counsel. I must also single out Dick Wentworth again—this time for the loan of his priceless Syd Glasso photos. Thanks to Ramon Vanden Brulle for his Foreward and, as always, to Kim, Mariah, Frank and the staff at Frank Amato Publications for their forbearance and support. I am thrilled to have my good friend, Jack Datisman's, painting as a cover. Finally, I'd like to tip my hat to all of the fly-fishers who came before us on the peninsula, most notably, Syd Glasso.

All inquiries should be addressed to:
Frank Amato Publications, Inc. • P.O. Box 82112 • Portland, Oregon 97282
503-653-8108 • www.amatobooks.com

Book & Cover Design: Mariah Hinds
Cover Artwork by Jack Datisman
ISBN-13: 978-1-57188-419-0
UPC: 0-81127-00253-5
Printed in Singapore

1 3 5 7 9 10 8 6 4 2

Table of Contents

Foreword

In the literature of angling, there are generally two types of authors, the ones who can write, and the ones who can fish. We read some of these fellows for what they can teach us about how to catch more or bigger fish; we read the others for what they can show us about this watery obsession we share, and maybe about ourselves. Doug Rose is the rare double threat, a thoughtful, observant, and skilled angler of deep experience, and an exceptionally talented and sensitive wordsmith. Simply, Doug brings it.

Rarer still, Doug is an angler who sincerely cares more for fish and the places they live than he does about his fishing. The pleasure he gains from the continued existence of wild fish and wild places does not begin and end with a solid hookset, and he understands that his satisfaction in a well-thrown loop or a beautiful surface take is necessarily compromised when the natural world is taking it on the chin. To an increasing number of outdoor enthusiasts, this way of thinking makes more and more sense, but Doug seems to have known it all along.

Not surprisingly, this attitude makes him a better writer, and perhaps just as unsurprisingly, it makes him a better angler. It is always rewarding to fish with Doug, or even just take a walk outside with him. A deep, carefully observed understanding of one's quarry and its habitats is bound to pay off, after all.

Find yourself with Doug on, say, a smallish Hood Canal salt marsh in the early autumn, thrashing through bulrushes, trying not to fall into muskrat holes, and you're bound to learn plenty about where and how to find some pretty sea-run cutthroat trout. It won't end there. Doug will teach you the names of the native forbs and grasses, or identify an unseen downy woodpecker by its voice and drum. The flattened patches of reeds you're casting from are not evidence of other anglers, they're otter landings, proven by the scat. We can admit that we really came for the dozen or so cutthroat, which Doug delivered handily, while acknowledging that he brought the silver platter too. This is the sort of thing we're talking about when we go on about the riches of the angling experience.

Washington's Olympic Peninsula offers Doug some opportunity to show off. It is literally his backyard. The Peninsula has seen its share of trouble. Its massive forest of giant hemlock, cedar, spruce, and fir looked to America like money lying on the ground, and we picked it up with ruthless efficiency. A couple of Peninsula rivers have been dammed to devastating effect for their wild fish. Commercial overharvest and poor hatchery management have not been a boon to local salmon and steelhead populations. But the Olympic Peninsula is a big, wild place, largely regulated and protected in national forests, national parks and marine reserves. It still shelters some of the most remote and pristine landscape in America, and its watersheds still gather some of the healthiest salmon and steelhead runs south of Alaska.

Doug knows what he has here, and he knows what it's worth. He's fished every part of the Peninsula, no small feat, from the trout streams and beaver ponds of its backcountry to its foaming surflines, from placid estuaries on Hood Canal to the muscular and legendary steelhead rivers of its coastal rain forests. He's cast flies over trout, char, salmon, steelhead, and rockfish, all the time keeping his writer's eye open, and paying very close attention.

Doug has engineered his life, not entirely without sacrifice, to fish, a lot, in of the last best places, a place he seems to have chosen relatively deliberately, a place he's chosen to love, and a place he's chosen to know, intimately. For pure fly-fishing hoopla, it might be easy to tick off a few venues more glamorous, arguably more productive. But for natural beauty, angling variety, elbow room, glimpses of the pristine, and year-round shots at wild, native fish, he could have chosen worse than the Olympic Peninsula. His choice is our boon, insofar as we take the opportunity to grasp his coattails.

The salient upshot here is that you could do much worse than go fishing with Doug Rose. Regrettably, not everybody can. I can't as much as I'd like. Fortunately we could do worse than read Doug Rose. Read, learn, enjoy.

—Ramon Vanden Brulle, 2007

Part I

Chapter One

A Sense of the Place

Dry-line time on the Quinault River.

How do you begin writing about fly-fishing on the Olympic Peninsula?

Well, I'm old enough to prefer story-telling to exposition, so let me tell you how I spent the last few days of October last year. It was the driest autumn on record. The rivers of the Quillayute System—the Sol Duc, Bogachiel, Calawah and Dickey—were warm trickles between fields of stones. That didn't prevent one of the best runs of hatchery summer steelhead in memory from returning to the lower Bogachiel and, ultimately, the "ponds" on the Calawah. Fly-fishers willing to hike away from the worm- and jig-fishermen took a lot of steelhead on dry lines, even waked and skated dry flies. The Hoh was low, too, but its glacial waters could still carry a boat, and summer-runs, chinook, and early silvers were all in the river at the same time.

I wasn't in the mood for crowds, though, so I focused on cutthroat. It was difficult on the Quillayute tributaries, but the deep pools held fish, silvery recent émigrés from the salt and amber-flanked, crimson-throated fish that had been in the river for a while. I had to work for them, had to hike and

Left: The Calawah River at low water.

wade long stretches of river to select pools, fish them carefully, then move on to a new hole. It is the kind of fishing I like, and one that Olympic Peninsula anglers have practiced for generations. I caught fat and lively cutthroat on the Sand Rock Hole on the Sol Duc and at Whale Rock on the Bogachiel. They hit the standard flies, the ones I've used for decades: the Spruce Fly and Knutson Spider, the Partridge and Orange soft hackle, and Royal Coachman Bucktails.

I would have been more than satisfied with the cutthroat and the chance for the odd summer steelhead on the West End rivers, but you don't have to settle for a single fishery on the Olympic Peninsula any time of year, let alone autumn. So I also spent a lot of time on the east side of the peninsula, fishing saltwater beaches for cutthroat and coho salmon. Sea-run cutthroat are available in the nearshore marine waters of the northeast Olympic "rain-shadow" year-round, and migrating coho move through these waters during September and October. Last fall, Admiralty Inlet and, especially, northern Hood Canal, were warmer than cutthroat and coho like. My good friend and expert coho beach fisherman, Ron Hirschi, had his worst year ever. The cutts were also tough, but I caught nice ones at Indian Island, Dabob Bay and Port Townsend Bay.

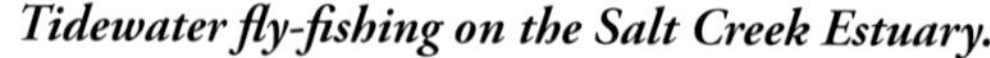

Olympic National Park contains the most extensive wilderness seashore in the lower 48 states.

The season in the upper portions of most rivers, creeks, and beaver ponds closes at the end of October, and that always sends me scrambling to my favorite ponds and tidal creeks one last time. Last autumn was the twentieth anniversary of finding my favorite beaver pond, actually a complex of ponds, on a tributary to the Big Quilcene River. I've taken a three-pound brook trout and many 15-plus-inch cutthroat from them, but they have fallen on hard times. The dams blew out about eight years ago, and the beavers that usually quickly repair them had disappeared. A new family of beavers finally patched the dams four years ago, and I caught a nearly 12-inch cutthroat in late October two years later. But when I returned the following June, Styrofoam worm containers and beer bottles littered the bank, and I saw no evidence of adult fish. I spent last fall on a beaver pond near the Hamma Hamma. I caught a chunky 15-inch brook trout, while my yellow Labrador retriever, Lily, rooted for frogs among the sedges.

I fished my favorite tidewater creek on Halloween day and was skunked for the first time in, oh I don't know, 15 years. That put me in a nasty mood, and I cursed the morons that had altered its flow in the name of salmon restoration. I tried to work when I got home, but I was restless and irritable. Knowing the upper Sol Duc,

Tidewater fly-fishing on the Salt Creek Estuary.

the portion in Olympic National Park, was only forty-five minutes away, I shut the computer down and headed west. The late-afternoon sun was only a few fingers above the tops of the fir trees by the time I hiked down to the river. I caught a nice resident rainbow, a mad head-over-teakettle jumper, on my third cast with a dark-bodied Knutson Spider. That was a much more satisfying way to end the season.

Of course, autumn is a sweet season for fly-fishing in many places. But March certainly isn't. Yet that is the best time to swing flies for the wild winter steelhead that return to the rivers that drain the Olympic Peninsula's windward, ocean-facing valleys, the region known as the West End. The Quillayute System and the Rain Forest's Quinault, Queets and Hoh rivers support the last relatively healthy complex of wild winter steelhead in the Pacific Northwest. They also routinely turn out many of the largest winter steelhead in the nation, some in excess of 30 pounds. These fish and these rivers were the inspirations for Syd Glasso's Spey flies, the most celebrated dressings to emerge from winter steelhead fly-fishing. Anglers from around the world make pilgrimages to these rivers each spring.

Trout are available in dozens of subalpine lakes in the Olympic Mountains.

Nor are steelhead the only springtime show on the Olympic Peninsula. After months of battering waves, the Pacific Coast surf settles down in spring, making it safer and more productive to cast for red-tailed surfperch at Kalaloch and Rialto Beach. Although it has been called an "island of rivers," many anglers eagerly anticipate the late-April opener on Price Lake, Anderson Lake, and Failor Lake. Those are small forested lakes, similar to dozens throughout the Pacific Northwest, but the peninsula's large, glacially-carved lakes also set it apart. Indeed, a recent report concluded that 50 lakes account for nearly 90 percent of all the surface water between Northern California and the Canadian border, and that 10,000-acre Lake Ozette contains nearly 20 percent of that water. If you add Lake Crescent and Lake Quinault, these three Olympic Peninsula lakes hold more than 40 percent of all the coastal surface water in all coastal lakes over 120 acres.

That leaves summer and winter. Summer is a good time for fly-fishing just about everywhere, but the Olympic Peninsula is one of the few places I know where salmon in salt water and trout in subalpine tarns swim within 20 miles of each other. If you have the energy, you can launch a boat in Port Angeles and fish the offshore rips for silvers on an August morning, and then hike into Lake Angeles and cast for brookies in the afternoon. As for winter, steelhead utterly dominate fly-fishing on the peninsula after the last pulse of late Satsop coho and Duckabush winter chum drift in from tidewater. But even that isn't entirely true, because I caught my largest cutthroat of the year, an 18-plus-inch bruiser, on December 5, 2005 on Dabob Bay.

You don't get this kind of diversity of species and run timing without a lot of different types of habitat. As is nearly always the case when it comes to fish distribution, geography and its creative process, geology, provide the explanations for the peninsula's fish. The land mass that became the Olympic Peninsula was created some 50 million years ago when a cataclysmic collision between the continental and oceanic tectonic plates thrust a huge chunk of the seafloor up onto the western edge of the coast. Over thousands of years, glaciers and weather worked and reworked the new land formation. The end product is a vaguely circular core of mountains, with river valleys radiating out from them in every direction. This labyrinth of peaks and canyons and river valleys astonished early explorers who were accustomed to linear mountain ranges like the Cascades and Coast Range,

" . . . after a toilsome march we reached the summit of Victor Pass, and here the scene changes," Lt. Joseph P. O'Neil wrote during the 1885 expedition that climbed the steep northern face of the Olympics near Port Angeles. "Looking east, west and south mountains, free from timber, some covered with snow, rise in wild, broken confusion."

The most obvious affect of this circular arrangement of mountains is an array of microclimates rather than the slight gradients of weather associated with north/south mountain ranges. When moisture-soaked weather systems from the Pacific Ocean hit the cold western flanks of the Olympic Mountains, they drop the bulk of their precipitation, as much as 140 inches annually, on the coast and West End valleys. This has created the peninsula's celebrated Hoh, Queets and Quinault Rain Forest valleys. Yet less than 40 miles away, on the leeward side of Mount Olympus and the Bailey Range, the Olympic "rain shadow" receives less than 14 inches of precipitation a year. In between these extremes, virtually every river valley and seashore experiences an essentially unique combination of rainfall, wind and light, and supports dramatically different ecosystems.

This plays itself out in a lot of different ways for fish, and by extension fly-fishers. The steady glacial flows of the Hoh, a Queets and Quinault allow sea-run cutthroat to migrate into them as early as mid-summer. But rain shadow creeks, like Bell Creek and Chimacum Creek, run very low in late summer and fall, and their cutthroat usually remain in the salt until winter rains bring up the creeks. Species such as chum and pink salmon, which spend little time in fresh water as juveniles but rear for extended periods in protected nearshore waters, thrive in the Rain Shadow's Dungeness Bay and Hood Canal's Dosewallips, Duckabush and Skokomish river estuaries. The big West End rivers' long mainstems and heavy flows are ideal for steelhead and chinook salmon, while the Dickey's and Satsop's many forks, tributaries and side channels are perfectly suited to coho.

For the angler, of course, the important thing is that all of these disparate yet proximate habitats, surrounded by tidewater on three sides and worked by the Pacific Northwest's relentless velvety rain for thousands of years, have combined to create one of the most diverse and compelling fly-fishing destinations in the world.

I took advantage of one of the peninsula's more obscure fisheries late one March. My friends were all fishing for steelhead on the West End, but early spring is also when newly-emerged chum salmon fry from Hood Canal rivers drop down to tidewater. Sea-run cutthroat prey on the fry aggressively, often selectively. I caught a snow-white 14-incher on my second cast with my chum fry pattern, the Keta Rose. I missed another fish, then hooked a real bruiser. It was an easy 20 inches, with thick shoulders and shimmering rose sides. It threw the hook. I rested the water for a moment. Little flocks of scaup flashed by so close I could see their blue bills, and I could hear pintails whistling in the saltmarsh. I tied on my friend, Jeffrey Delia's, Conehead Squid, for a change of pace. A 16-inch cutt hit it on my first cast.

That's a pretty good way to spend a couple hours on a cold March morning as far as I'm concerned.

Swinging wet flies for sea-runs on the East Fork of the Satsop.

Chapter Two

Salmonid Crossroads

Fluvial cutthroat spend their entire lives in the river.

Outside the Olympic mudminnow, a 2-inch river-dweller most abundant between the Queets and Grays Harbor, no fish species are found only on the peninsula, and even up the Chehalis to the Skookumchuck River. And with the exception of its widely-heralded winter steelhead runs, the peninsula doesn't necessarily offer the most productive fly-fishing for most West Coast fish. More summer steelhead return to the North Umpqua and Deschutes, and more chinook return to the Rogue River. More chum salmon spawn in the small, muddy creeks and rivers of southern Puget Sound, and the Skagit and Snohomish systems have more bull trout and pink salmon. Mountain lake fishing is at least as good in the Cascades and Sierras, and anyone who really wants to catch a sockeye on the fly should head for Alaska. The same goes for coho and big wild resident rainbows.

> "All fish out here that are worth their salt came from the ocean."
>
> —*Dick Wentworth*

That leaves coastal cutthroat. Although there are larger runs to some north Puget Sound rivers, I wouldn't trade the peninsula's cutthroat fishery for anyplace in the world. Cutthroat are available year-round on some Hood Canal and Admiralty Inlet beaches, and the number of 15-plus-inch fish has increased substantially since the Washington Department of Fish and Wildlife (WDFW) implemented catch-and-release regulations for them in salt water. You can also catch them on big rivers like the Queets and Quillayute during summer, and in virtually every creek, stream, and estuary in autumn. You can fish for resident cutthroat in backcountry creeks and beaver ponds, and for Lake Crescent's unique crescenti cutthroat, which have reached 12 pounds.

Besides its winter steelhead and cutthroat, the thing that really distinguishes the Olympic Peninsula from other West Coast fly-fishing destinations is that it is in a very real sense a "salmonid crossroads." It is as far south as you find substantial runs of pink salmon and, with the exception of interior races, the peninsula is near the southern end of the range of native char and sockeye salmon. On the other hand, the Olympic Peninsula and Vancouver Island are at the northern end of the range of native coastal stocks of summer steelhead. These fish are genetically different from Columbia/Snake stocks and the much larger "fall" summer-runs of British Columbia's interior basins. The Olympics and Vancouver Island also seem to have been near the northernmost reach of the "half-pounder" life history of summer steelhead, which have all but vanished in recent decades.

That such a lavish assemblage of salmonids would be so close together is remarkable, but the fact that the very best fly-fishing on the Olympic Peninsula focuses on wild fish in their natural setting is the thing that makes this place truly unique. You can't say that about most celebrated trout-fishing destinations in the lower 48 states. Introduced brown and rainbow trout provide the bulk of the sport, even in the West's cutthroat country. Nor can you say it about many steelhead rivers, where hatchery fish provide put-and-take angling over shattered wild runs. There are extensive releases of hatchery steelhead and salmon on the Olympic Peninsula, but the best fly-fishing is for native fish in their ancestral habitats. It's for West End steelhead in March, and late-summer coho in the ocean. It's for cutthroat over Hood Canal oyster bars in September and late chum over mud flats in December. It's for Elwha rainbows and Lake Crescent Beardslee and crescenti trout.

Summer chinook are available on the larger West End rivers.

Chinook: With fish reaching 50-plus pounds today and documented 100-pounders from the Elwha River before the construction of its dams, chinook are the region's largest salmon. Olympic Peninsula chinook, which are also known locally as "kings," display three different life histories: spring, summer (spring/summer stocks are often lumped together) and fall. Entering fresh water between late February and May, springers spawn higher in the river than later-returning chinook. They are only found in large systems like the Queets, Quinault, Hoh and, historically, the Elwha. Summer and spring/summer stocks are more widely distributed, and are native to the Satsop, Bogachiel, Dungeness and Skokomish. Fall kings are the most abundant and are found in rivers as small as the Hoko and Hoquiam. Currently, the strongest chinook returns are to the large rain forest rivers and Grays Harbor/Chehalis tributaries. All Hood Canal and eastern Strait of Juan de Fuca stocks are listed as "threatened" under the Endangered Species Act (ESA). The Sol Duc hosts the only spring chinook fishing, and it is largely an introduced hatchery run. Summer and spring/summer kings are available in the Quillayute System rivers and Hoh, but not that many fly-fishers pursue them because they adopt deep, difficult-to-reach holding lies and tend to be dour. Fall chinook are more aggressive and will hit large, deeply-fished leeches. There has been little salt water fly-fishing for chinook in Olympic Peninsula waters to date, but it presents opportunity when the seasons are open and fish are available.

Coho Salmon: Coho spawn in more Olympic Peninsula rivers than any other salmonid except cutthroat trout. Fly-fishers catch them in salt water, estuaries, and large rivers and creeks. Silvers, as they are also commonly known, range between 6 and 18 pounds, but 20-pounders are taken. Coho spawners are all three-year-olds, except sexually precocious males referred to as "jacks," which return a year early. Salt water anglers take bright coho in the Pacific Ocean, Strait of Juan de Fuca, Admiralty Inlet and Hood Canal from midsummer into September, with the larger "hook-nosed" fish arriving latest. Most silvers enter fresh water in October and November. Degraded habitat and over fishing have reduced the run sizes on many small streams, and most creeks are now closed to salmon fishing. The Satsop was famous for its 20-pounders and for bright fish that arrived into January. With its sprawling forks and low-gradient wetlands and side channels, the Dickey River was also a very productive coho system. The Sol Duc has a race of "summer coho" that drifts into the lower river in August and September. The large West End rivers and the Grays Harbor/Chehalis river tributaries still host strong populations of wild and hatchery fish. The Dungeness River's hatchery run is the rain shadow's most productive, and anglers take as many as 4,000 fish annually. In salt water, coho hit baitfish imitations stripped rapidly along tide rips and around the edges of bird works. Beach anglers catch silvers during late summer at Point Wilson and Marrowstone Point. Coho are more difficult to entice in estuaries but will hit spider and soft-hackle flies fished on long leaders and clear intermediate lines. They become aggressive again in fresh water and will bite bright attractor patterns.

Chum Salmon: Chum are the second-largest Pacific salmon, typically ranging between 7 and 14 pounds, and are the most abundant salmon in Washington. They usually spawn in the lower reaches of rivers and creeks. Three different races of chum salmon are native to the peninsula: summer, fall, and "late." Currently listed as "threatened" under the ESA, summer chum are found in the larger rain shadow and Hood Canal rivers and enter fresh water in August and September. Fall chum, which arrive during October and November, are by far the most abundant, and their numbers have been enhanced by large hatchery releases on many Hood Canal and lower Chehalis River tributaries. Late chum don't leave salt water until late November or early December and are native to Hood Canal's Skokomish, Hamma Hamma, Dosewallips, Duckabush, and Big Quilcene rivers. Juvenile chum salmon drop down to the estuaries almost immediately after they emerge in spring. They spend up to two months in estuaries and nearshore shallows before migrating to the ocean. Coastal estuaries are smaller and feature much smaller chum populations than those of Hood Canal and Rain Shadow streams, with the exception of the Quinault River, which has a large estuary and chum run. Most chum spend between three and five years at sea. They provide excellent sport in salt water, and have also become very popular on the Satsop and other lower Chehalis River tributaries. The state record is a 25-pound Satsop fish that was caught in 1997.

John McMillan with Hoh coho.

Pink Salmon: Also known as humpies, because of the large growth that develops on the backs of spawning adult males, pink salmon average around 4 pounds. All pinks have a two-year life-cycle, and on the peninsula they only return during odd-numbered years. There are "summer" and "autumn" races of pinks, but the Dungeness River is the only Olympic stream that still has a summer run. Summer fish return during August and early September and spawn in the upper Dungeness and Graywolf rivers. Small runs of fall pinks enter some coastal rivers, but the strongest runs occur on Rain Shadow and western Hood Canal rivers. Pinks are similar to chum in that they use fresh water almost exclusively for spawning and incubation, and drift down to salt water as soon as they emerge from the gravel. Juveniles linger in estuaries during spring. The Dungeness, Dosewallips, Duckabush, and Hamma Hamma support the largest runs today, and they all have large bays or estuaries. Historically, an estimated 400,000 pinks spawned in the Elwha every other year, but they have been extirpated from the system. After they return to the rivers, pinks like to hole up in deep pools until they are ready to spawn. There are currently no legal pink fisheries in Olympic Peninsula rivers, but anglers catch them regularly in saltwater during July and August. They are usually taken slightly deeper than coho and like cerise or hot pink flies.

Sockeye: The vast majority of sockeye salmon return to river systems that contain a large lake. Most spawn along lake margins or in tributaries, and rear for a year or two in the lake before migrating to sea. The Quinault Tribe's Lake Quinault sockeye were internationally celebrated during the late 19th century, and the commercial name for all salmon then, "Quinnaut," derived from the word Quinault. Most sockeye spend two years at sea and return as 5- to 8-pound adults. Lake Quinault sockeye return in spring, while Lake Ozette fish appear between late spring and midsummer, and Sol Duc sockeye enter the river in June and July. Large runs of sockeye historically returned to the Elwha's Lake Sutherland, the North Fork of the Skokomish's Lake Cushman, and the Dickey River's Dickey Lake, but they are all functionally extinct. Landlocked sockeye are known as kokanee. They naturally occur in Lake Crescent and provide the bulk of the diet for the lake's large Beardslee and crescenti trout. Kokanee have been planted in many lowland lakes to provide sport fisheries but are difficult to entice on flies. The Sol Duc is the only river where you can currently fish for sockeye and they are concentrated downstream of Lake Creek, the outlet to Lake Pleasant. The best way to tempt them remains something of a mystery, but they seem to prefer small blue-and-silver flies fished in pools with a slow jigging retrieve.

Rainbow Trout

Winter Steelhead: The anadromous form of rainbow trout, steelhead, specifically winter steelhead, are the Olympic Peninsula's signature fly-fishing attraction today. As steelhead

The Olympic Peninsula's ultimate prize—a large winter steelhead on the fly.

runs have foundered in other regions, the wild winter fish of the West End's major rivers have remained relatively robust. There have been recent declines on the glacial rivers and early fishing closures on the Queets and Hoh. But compared to other Pacific Northwest rivers, the steelhead of the Quillayute System and rain forest rivers are in good shape. Besides turning out more wild fish, West End rivers also produce some of the largest winter steelhead in the world. This is a function of these steelhead's tendency to remain at sea—and continue growing—longer than other stocks. More than 40 percent of Quillayute winter steelhead spend three or more years in salt water. This translates into lots of 20-pound fish, and fish larger than 30 pounds have been caught in the Sol Duc, Bogachiel and Quinault within the last few years. Steelhead as large as 37 pounds have been taken in tribal nets on the Queets and Hoh. Historically, as many as 35 percent of wild winter fish arrived between late November and the middle of January, but today the bulk of the wild run appears in February and March. The loss of the early component of the run is the result of incidental overharvest of early-timed wild fish by tribal and sport anglers pursuing hatchery steelhead. Hatchery steelhead from Chambers Creek stock have been planted in most West End rivers not controlled by the tribes, and they return in December and January, as do tribal hatchery runs on the Hoh, Queets and Quinault.

Summer Steelhead: Research suggests that Olympic Peninsula coastal summer steelhead are more closely related to coastal winter steelhead than Columbia/Snake or other interior populations of summer steelhead. Whatever their provenance, summer-runs are native to far fewer Olympic Peninsula rivers than winter fish, and hatchery runs have been established in only a handful of rivers. Anglers historically took wild summer steelhead from Hood Canal rivers such as the Skokomish and Duckabush and Rain Shadow systems like the Dungeness and Elwha, but these populations have all but disappeared. Currently, the strongest wild stocks are found in the Quillayute System and rain forest rivers, and surveys indicate that these populations have declined precipately in recent years. Wild West End steelhead are usually fairly small, typically ranging between 4 and 10 pounds, and are deep-bodied and short. They enter fresh water from early summer through autumn, and swim deep into the backcountry, where they hold in shady pools and canyons until spawning in late winter or spring. Most summer steelhead angling on the peninsula today focuses on Skamania stock hatchery fish, which range from 6 to 15 pounds and have more streamlined bodies than natives. Skamania smolts have been released from the Lyre to the Dungeness and from the Humptulips to the Sol Duc. More recently, hatchery releases have been halted on the Dungeness, Elwha and Humptulips to protect beleaguered wild runs. The largest remaining hatchery runs are to the Wynoochee and Calawah, and the Calawah and lower Bogachiel are best suited for fly-fishing. Hatchery steelhead are taken from June into October, with June the best month on the Wynoochee and July on the Calawah.

Resident Rainbow: Most Olympic Peninsula rainbow trout that have access to salt water are anadromous, and migrate to sea after two or three years in fresh water as juveniles. However, small numbers of resident rainbows are found in most major river systems, and they were abundant in the Elwha before and during the first few decades after the dams were built. These were true resident fish, reaching several pounds, and not simply 7- or 8-inch smolts that anglers called "trout." The upper Sol Duc also supported good numbers of resident rainbow, and anglers like Dick Wentworth and

Don Kaas took them in fast water on dry flies. "We called it 'riffle-popping'," Wentworth said. Resident rainbow are also available above waterfalls on some large rivers, but many of these fish are the result of earlier stocking efforts. However, a recent report by ONP suggests that rainbow in the upper Dosewallips may be a population that was established before glacial activity created the falls that now blocks migratory fish. The peninsula's most famous resident rainbow trout are Lake Crescent's renowned Beardslee trout, which commonly weigh 10 pounds and have reached more than 20. Beardslees are descended from steelhead blocked from the ancestral lake's outlet to the Elwha by a landslide, and they have adapted to the large, cold infertile lake by becoming deep-swimming kokanee predators.

Coastal Cutthroat (*Oncorhynchus clarkii clarkii*): Cutthroat trout are found in more Olympic Peninsula rivers and creeks than any other salmonid species, and they display the most diverse and complex life histories of any native trout. The anadromous form, sea-run cutthroat, are most well known and abundant. They are found on Rain Shadow creeks like Chimacum Creek and glacial torrents like the Queets. Most spend a couple of years in fresh water, then drop down to salt water for several months of feeding. They can make repeated journeys to salt water, and often move between fresh and tidewater in search of food. Juvenile cutthroat native to coastal systems tend to remain in fresh water longer than Rain Shadow fish, and their saltwater sojourns are shorter, often bringing them back to the river by early autumn. Rain Shadow rivers usually have low autumn flows and protected estuaries, and cutthroat from the eastern strait, Admiralty Inlet and Hood Canal may linger in tidewater through early winter or longer. The average sea-run is about a foot long, but fish approaching 20 inches are taken. Cutthroat that remain in large river systems but migrate within them are called fluvial, and are most common on larger rivers. Adfluvial cutthroat spawn in streams but spend most of their adult life in lakes. Lake Crescent's "crescenti" cutthroat are adfluvial, as are some Lake Ozette and Lake Quinault fish. Adfluvial cutthroat attain the greatest size, and the record crescenti is a 12-pound fish. Cutthroat have larger mouths and more teeth than rainbows of comparable size and they feed more readily on other fish. Resident cutthroat are most common above barriers and in small headwater creeks. They have larger spots, are usually darker, and they seldom reach 10 inches. Cutthroat spawn higher in the watershed than any other salmonid except native char.

Native Char: Char are different from North American trout in that they spawn in autumn rather than spring and have light spotting on a dark background rather than dark spots. Dolly Varden and bull trout are both found on the Olympic Peninsula, and since it is impossible to tell them apart in the field, the term "native char" has become popular short-hand. Char favor large cold systems for spawning, and were historically abundant in the Skokomish, Dungeness, Elwha, Hoh, Queets and Quinault. Large char are efficient predators, and can reach 10 pounds. Many early anglers claimed char did serious harm to juvenile salmon and eggs, while characteristically absolving themselves of responsibility for the effects of splash damming, irrigation diversions, and impassible dams. Char require colder, cleaner water than even trout, and they spawn higher in a watershed than any salmonid. Today Olympic Peninsula bull trout are listed under the ESA. Recent research by ONP's Sam Brenkman has revealed that many Hoh River bull trout are anadromous, with extremely complex life histories. One tagged female spent several years in the river, dropped down to salt water, entered a

A Queets River summer steelhead.

An impressive male sea-run cutthroat.

different river, returned to the Hoh, then repeated the process. On the North Fork of the Skokomish, bull trout spawn and rear in the river, but spend time as adults feeding in Lake Cushman. Some char remain in headwater areas for extended periods, perhaps their entire lives, and these brightly-colored 5- to 8-inch fish were called "glacier trout" by early anglers.

Brook Trout: Native to East Coast and Great Lakes basins, brook trout, which are actually a char, have become a double-edged sword on the Olympic Peninsula. They were among the first "trout" carried into the Olympic backcountry, and in *Fishing in the Olympics* E.B. Webster reported 85,000 were planted in the upper Sol Duc and Deer Lake in 1922. They are capable of spawning successfully over a wider range of habitats and conditions than native trout, and today you find them in mountain lakes, beaver ponds, and headwater streams. Without them, many high-elevation lakes would offer no fishing whatsoever. However, brook trout have a tendency to stunt in mountain lakes that have an abundance of food and few predators. Even worse, they can successfully spawn with native char, but the offspring of these liaisons are sterile. The park has found brook trout in headwater rivers below lakes on the North Fork Skokomish, Elwha, Dungeness, Grand Creek and in lakes that drain into the Hoh.

Mountain Whitefish: The state-record mountain whitefish is over 5 pounds, but most Olympic Peninsula fish are less than one pound. They are most abundant on the large rain forest rivers, and feed on nymphs, small crustaceans and, occasionally, fish. They readily hit flies, and anglers can spice up an otherwise slow day by dead-drifting small nymphs. Whitefish tend to favor riffles and runs during summer and gang up in pools during winter. Most good whitefish water is in ONP, where they are protected under catch-and-release regulations, and you must fish single-hook, barbless flies.

Marine Fish

Rockfish: You can call them rock cod, sea bass or red snapper, but the most accurate common name for members of the Scorpaenidae family is rockfish. They range in size from 2-pound copper rockfish to 20-plus-pound yelloweye rockfish. For fly-fishers, the black rockfish of the coast and western Strait of Juan de Fuca is the most important species. They range from 1 to 4 pounds, and are among the best-tasting salt water fish. They are abundant between spring and early autumn around nearshore kelp beds, and will hit everything from Clouser Minnows to white Bunny Leeches. Rockfish are schooling fish and when you catch one you will usually catch more. The presentation is as simple as it gets—cast close to the kelp with a sink-tip line and let the fly sink naturally. Black rockfish tend to suspend in middle depths, and strikes usually come on the drop. Occasionally rockfish swarm on the surface during late spring or early summer, and can be caught on poppers. Neah Bay, La Push and the waters west of Sekiu have the healthiest nearshore rockfish populations in the state. Copper and quillback rockfish are the most common rockfish in the eastern strait, Admiralty Inlet and Hood Canal, but populations have plummeted. All marine bottomfish are off limits in Hood Canal, and the daily limit of rockfish in Admiralty Inlet and the eastern strait is one fish. That makes mounting a fishing trip for them rather ridiculous, because they don't survive catch-and-release well. The "scorpion" in the rockfish's taxonomic name refers to the toxins they carry in spines on their fins. Be careful handling them because it really hurts if you get stung.

Red-tailed Surfperch: Sandy beaches are the homes of these scrappy shallow-water perch, and Olympic Peninsula fly-fishers take them near Copalis Beach and Moclips, South Beach, Kalaloch, Beach 4, Rialto Beach, and small remote beaches on the north and south coastal strips. Ranging from 1 to around 3 pounds, perch school in the troughs and depressions that run parallel to the beach, and are taken on high tides by wading anglers. Intermediate and sink-tip lines are popular, and orange, yellow, and red "shrimp" and "crab" patterns are effective. Surfperch apparently haunt the sandy beaches year round, but the surf is safest for wading between late March and early October. Even then, it is critical to pay attention to the waves and tide. Much of the surf-perch beach on the peninsula is within the boundaries of Olympic National Park, and anglers should consult park regulations.

Flounder and Sole: Not many fly-fishers target flatfish, but several species of shallow-water sole and flounder provide fine sport on light rods and excellent table fare. Hood Canal's myriad pocket coves and mud flats are superb flatfish habitat, but all bottomfish in the canal are protected now due to die-offs related to low oxygen content. However, Dungeness Bay, Sequim Bay, Fresh Water Bay, and Port Townsend Bay remain open to bottomfishing, and each contains populations of starry flounder, rock sole, and sand sole. Starry flounder are the largest, reaching nearly 20 pounds, although they are usually only a pound or two. They are abundant over mud sand bottoms in the intertidal zone and will hit flies that imitate shrimp, crabs, or small fish. Most common over sandy bottoms, sand sole are usually less than 1 pound, and can be identified by fin rays at the front of their dorsal fin that aren't connected with rest of the fin membrane. Rock sole are about the same size as sand sole, but prefer gravel bottoms and their sides have a rough, "sandpapery" feel. Both rock and sand sole will hit small shrimp and baitfish patterns fished along the bottom on sink-tip or full-sinking lines.

Bull trout (shown) and Dolly Varden are the Olympic Peninsula's only native char.

Chapter Three

The Royal Coachman Chronicles

Syd Glasso swinging a Spey fly on the Sol Duc.

It's easy for newcomers and visitors to imagine that fly-fishing is still in something of an embryonic state on the Olympic Peninsula. Lake Crescent's large Beardslee and crescenti trout attracted anglers from as far away as Great Britain by the early 1900s. Since the end of World War II, the chinook and coho that pass down the Strait of Juan de Fuca each summer and the winter steelhead that return to West End rivers have drawn thousands of anglers annually. Until recently, however, you could have fished Lake Crescent or Sekiu or Forks for a lifetime and not seen more than a handful of fly-rods. Even now, if you avoid places like the middle Elwha, Price Lake, and the Calawah's "ponds" when summer steelhead are around, you won't see many fly-fishers.

This is what Enos Bradner had to say about Olympic Peninsula fly-fishing in his classic 1950 volume, *Northwest Angling*: "In the section of the ocean highway south of Forks leading down to Aberdeen are several rivers that would be shrines in the hearts of anglers everywhere if their possibilities were nationally known."

Bradner also wrote, "All of the Olympic Peninsula rivers have fine runs of winter fish and most of them should show some good fly-fishing. While the fly is used very sparingly in these streams and some of the water is not suitable for the artificials, there exist long drifts where a fly would work. These streams present the only virgin steelhead fly water left on the West Coast and some Ike Walton can make himself famous by pioneering an exploration of their possibilities."

Actually, Bradner wrote those words after just such a steelheader had already appeared. He was Syd Glasso, of course, the Forks school teacher who in the 1950s single-handedly adapted Scottish Spey flies to Pacific Northwest steelhead rivers. Meticulous and inspired, Glasso was a true artist, and his Sol Duc and Heron series married the motion and design of the Scottish originals like the Lady Caroline with hotter steelhead colors and new materials. They proved not only effective on winter steelhead, they have enthralled subsequent generations of fly tiers. Glasso was also an excellent caster and deep wader, and he built his own lead-coated fly lines to get his flies down to the peninsula's bottom-hugging winter fish.

Of course, winter steelhead are a formidable challenge on fly tackle, especially the gear available during Glasso's day, and he once said that in 20 years he only saw six other anglers who seriously pursued them with flies on West End rivers. Trout were an entirely different matter. Local and visiting anglers have been catching them with flies in the Olympics for a long time. Indeed, fly rods were standard fishing tackle during the mid to late 19th century, and many Olympic explorers and pioneers had a working knowledge of East Coast dressings like the Brown Hackle, Professor, Mosquito, and, especially, Royal Coachman. Early anglers used fly-rods to fish both flies and bait, and they were standard gear among trout anglers until monofilament line and spinning tackle came on the scene in the 1950s.

"Tried a cast in a lovely pool above camp and was happy to see a beauty rise to my first cast," James Christie, leader of the first group of explorers to cross the Olympic Mountains, wrote of a day fishing the Elwha in 1890. "Another twenty feet of line was run out and gently dropping a "Professor" and "Royal Coachman" beneath the shadow on the rock opposite, in a trice I had struck a fish. A fish that would fight, my first salmon trout on the Elwha. I landed him after five minutes of careful angling, the fish fighting to the end. Then followed one half hour of as fine fishing as any I ever enjoyed on the thousand streams I have had the pleasure of fishing in, carrying to camp fourteen splendid trout; weight about forty pounds, no mean basket from any water."

The Age of Exploration

The first settlers began trickling into the Olympic Peninsula lowlands in the 1850s, but as the 19th century drew to a close, the peninsula's mountainous interior remained the West's last major unexplored wilderness. I have no doubt that some early settlers caught trout on flies long before Christie and other explorers ventured into the backcountry, but the farmers and miners and early loggers left scant written record of their angling. On the other hand, the adventurers and scientific and military men who built trails and charted maps in the region in the 1880s and '90s were encouraged to record their observations, and many were fly-fishermen.

It is fun reading the portions of the explorers' journals that describe fly-fishing in the backcountry, both for the documentation of early fly-fishing and to get glimpses of the unimaginable historic abundance of Olympic Peninsula fish. The first reference to fly-fishing that I have seen was by Lt. Joseph P. O'Neil, a young Notre Dame graduate stationed in Port Townsend. During the summer of 1885, O'Neil led a military expedition into the mountains that loom over Port Angeles. They camped by Ennis Creek, "a beautiful stream clear and cold and filled with trout." On a day off, one of the men went fishing, and O'Neil wrote, " . . . with his rod and fly secured a fine mess of trout and in crossing got a good ducking by losing his footing."

Known as the Press Expedition because it accepted the challenge of Seattle newspapers to become the first Euro-Americans to cross the Olympic Mountains, Christie's party hiked up the Elwha and down the Quinault rivers during the winter of 1889-90. Christie was an avid fly-fisher, and he caught his trout in Geyser Valley, the flats between Rica Canyon and the Grand Canyon of the Elwha. Historians have identified these fish, which he called "salmon-trout," as steelhead, but I'm not sure. Their size, "between three and four pounds," is small for winter fish, and you seldom encounter such compliant concentrations of steelhead. I suspect they were bull trout, and recently Sam Brenkman, Olympic National Park's head fisheries biologist, told me also thinks they were most likely native char.

Of all the explorers, Professor Louis F. Henderson may have been the most devoted fly-fisher. A member of Lt. O'Neil's second Olympic expedition, which explored the southeast Olympics during the summer of 1890, Henderson was a trained botanist. He spent his days collecting and preserving plants, but seems to have devoted every spare hour to fly-fishing. "Proff. Henderson was so interested in fishing, despite the rain that continued falling all day, that we had trouble getting him into his meals," Private Harry Fisher observed in his journal. "But thanks to his rod and success as a fisherman the camp was well supplied with trout of the finest quality." Henderson's journal noted that Lake Cushman's trout "take the fly readily" and "I was always very successful, especially toward evening, for fish are abundant in the lake, both brook-trout and "bull trout."

Professor Henderson left the mountains before the end of the summer, but Private Fisher continued to chronicle the fishing. "There seemed to be but one size of trout," he wrote of an evening on the North Fork Skokomish, near Camp 2. "Each and every one was the picture of the first caught, weighing 2 1/2 pounds. A very large brook trout, and to land one trout, dear reader, repaid us for all the day's work. Such trout as those and in such a place was worthy the angling of gods of old. Leaping a foot into the air, they took the fly from above, and in no single instance did they ever miss taking a good hold of the hook." On the Humptulips, he wrote, "leaving Danton to keep house, I cast with great success, landing fifteen trout for supper . . ." The next day's journal read: "We again employed the rod to good use, landing thirty-five trout."

The Era of Resorts and Hiking

It didn't take long for word of the Olympic Peninsula's extraordinary fishing to spread. By 1910, anglers had 11 fishing resorts to choose from on Lake Crescent. Most of the fishing for its large Beardslee and crescenti trout was done with lures, specifically a silver spoon that was trolled deep with fine copper line. But smaller trout were the focus at other resorts, and many anglers pursued them with flies. The Hot Springs Resorts on the Sol Duc and Boulder Creek, a tributary of the Elwha, advertised their fishing. My friend, Ron Hirschi's great great grandfather, Tom Pierce, was one of the first settlers at the mouth of the Duckabush River on Hood Canal. One of his sons built a resort on the north side of the river.

"When my father would come up for weekends," Douglas Eagen recalled in the *Port Townsend Leader* in 1912, "we three would go the Duckabush . . . My father, something of a fly-fisherman, would cast right on the ripple he wanted for a hungry trout and I there learned something about fly-fishing. I would carry his creel and we would go home loaded with beautiful trout, enough for our breakfast and some left over for the others."

Unlike today, when most anglers expect to be able to drive or boat to a fishing destination, hiking was considered a normal adjunct to angling in the early 20th century. Within a score of years of Christie's and O'Neil's expeditions, a network of trails provided access to the Olympic foothills and high country. Backcountry shelters were common and a three-story lodge was built in Enchanted Valley, on the East Fork of the Quinault. The first hatchery trout were carried into Olympic Mountain lakes, which were largely fishless, during the 1920s, and non-native species such as eastern brook and Montana black-spotted cutthroat (westslope cutthroat) were widely distributed in both lakes and streams.

The upper Elwha River was the premier fly-fishing destination for early hikers in the Olympics, as it is today. This is how E. B. Webster described the river in his 1922 volume, *Fishing the Olympics*, ". . . it is in the Elwha, with its succession of canyons, its boiling whirlpools, its swift currents, its millions of boulders, its almost constant whitewater, that the Rainbow finds its true environment . . . From rapids to rapids and pool to pool they (fly-fishers) follow the course of the river, climbing up and around canyons and again on, till the day is far spent, picking out a good trout here and there, releasing those that are undersized—catching fish as a zest to recreation."

An anecdote about Herb Crisler illustrates the popularity of fly-fishing in the Olympic Peninsula in the years preceding World War II. Known today for his and his wife,

Dick Wentworth at the oars on the Sol Duc.

Lois's, popular documentary "Olympic Elk," Crisler spent much of his life in the Olympics. During the summer of 1930, he bet a Seattle newspaper that he could survive in the Olympics for 30 days entirely on food that he could kill and forage. It proved to be more difficult than Crisler anticipated, and after several weeks he was weak and desperate for a solid meal. Then, dropping down from Queets Basin to the Elwha near Chicago Camp, he found discarded potato peelings, a leader, and fly stuck in a tree. This was more than 20 miles from the Elwha trailhead. He cut a willow for a pole and put the fly to quick work. He caught a dozen rainbows, and cooked nine of them with the potato peelings.

"Delicious," he wrote.

Local Knowledge

As the Olympic Peninsula's population grew and the amenities of civilization created more leisure time, the number of home-grown anglers who fly-fished increased. The first road around the Olympics was completed in the 1930s, and a high-clearance Model A Ford let anglers explore roads that you wouldn't dream of in a contemporary sedan. Newspapers began to report on angling, especially on opening day and when large fish were taken. Many long-time local residents alive today received richly detailed accounts of this early Olympic Peninsula fly-fishing from their parents and grandparents.

"My dad, Bill Wentworth, caught a spring chinook on a number 6 Royal Coachman Bucktail in the Sol Duc in the early 1930s," Dick Wentworth remembers. "It was June or July and he caught it in the Sand Rock Hole. Dad also used to sometimes fly-fish for trout in July on the upper Sol Duc during the 1950s. My uncle, Glenn 'Mickey' Merchant, had 40 acres on the Calawah. He packed Montana black-spotted cutthroat into mountain lakes. Uncle Mick mostly used a size 4 or 5 nickle/copper spinner and strip of bullhead meat for cutthroat. He called it the 'meat axe.'" But he fished flies for cutthroat once in a while. He would use a Royal Coachman and a Mosquito dropper."

Although he is best known as Syd Glasso's talented protégé and creator of the Mr. Glasso and Quillayute Spey flies, Dick Wentworth had begun fly-fishing by the time he got to know Glasso. "I was introduced to fly-fishing by my principal, Mr. Irwin Edwards," Dick said. "He took us down to Sylvia Lake when I was 12 or 13. He had an old Herter's bamboo rod and he let me use it one time. Those rainbows really liked the fly. I got the book *Trout* from the library and my mom got me the *Family Circle Book of Trout Flies*. Later, Syd was my junior high school teacher. He taught English and study hall then and sometimes he would tie a trout fly in study hall to inspire us. When I got about 16 or 17, it became too easy taking winter runs on bait, and that's when I beat on Syd's door."

Don Kaas grew up in Port Angeles and began fly-fishing Lake Crescent and the Elwha in the 1940s. "My uncle used to the run the lokey (logging train) for Bloedel," he said, "and we would go out during grouse and deer season and ride the train up the East Fork of the Dickey. It was really good cutthroat fishing and there was a big beaver pond on Skunk Creek with cutthroat. Chick Lynne used to put on fly-casting demonstrations at the high school," he said. "He ran a sporting goods store and sandwich shop in town. He would have someone stand and hold their hand out and he would lay the fly in the palm of their hand from 50 or 60 feet away. His favorite fly was the Blue Upright and he liked to fish for the rainbow/cutthroat hybrids in the North Fork of the Sol Duc."

During the 1960s, Kaas took his family to the Sol Duc near the current Sappho Hatchery just before school reopened in the fall. "It's a nice spot and I had a fire going," he said. "This guy comes along and says, 'Do you mind if I fish here?' It was Syd Glasso. Afterwords I gave him a cup of coffee. I didn't have any idea who he was then. I used to run into him a couple of times a year after that. He gave me four flies. They were kind of like Speys on number 4 hooks. I used them up."

Les Johnson needs no introduction in a book on fly-fishing in the Pacific Northwest. Growing up in Aberdeen in the 1950s, he spent his early years chasing cutthroat, steelhead and salmon on Gray's Harbor rivers and creeks. "A lot of Gary's Harbor anglers fly-fished for sea-run cutthroat in those days," Les recalled. "I purchased my first fly-fishing outfit from Reiner's Sporting Goods, which was primarily a pawn shop on Wishkah Street in Aberdeen. It was a used but well-kept Granger bamboo with a 3 3/8-inch Hardy Perfect reel and a double-taper silk line. Failor's Sporting Goods was also in Aberdeen and a great sporting goods store. Failor's had an excellent fly-fishing department with all of the popular cutthroat flies of the day, including the Faulk, a very popular local pattern that is featured in my cutthroat book."

According to Johnson, the Gray Hackle Peacock, Gray Hackle Yellow, Gray Hackle Red and Knutson Spider (red, yellow or black bodied) were also popular on Grays Harbor rivers during the 1950s. "The Knutson Spider was one of the very few Stillaguamish flies we used, that gained such popularity during that period," he said. "And there were a lot of tiers in Grays Harbor who cranked out a huge variety of nameless patterns that were successful for cutts and steelhead."

Glasso

Although Syd Glasso was not the first person to take winter fish on flies in the Olympics—Webster wrote of fly-fishers using "bass flies" for them in his 1920s—he was almost certainly the first to do it on a regular basis and with patterns of his own design. Outside of the Olympic Peninsula,

Glasso's reputation today rests entirely on his Spey flies, but a number of local anglers remember him as a man and teacher and, most of all, as a truly extraordinary fly-fisherman. According to Dick Wentworth, Glasso routinely filled a 30-fish steelhead punchcard during the 1950s, and the season often ended in February then, not April as it does today. He also caught large fish, including an 18-pound, 12-ounce winter fish that won the 1958 *Field & Stream* steelhead fly-fishing category.

As attractive as Glasso's flies are to both winter steelhead and anglers, they would not have been effective unless he could get them down to winter steelhead. During the 1950s, Scientific Anglers' Wet Cell lines, full-sinking line coated with nylon, were the most advanced on the market, but they were no match for the peninsula's steep, fast, rain-swollen rivers. Glasso urged the manufacturers to develop faster-sinking lines for winter steelhead, and when they didn't, he created his own sinking heads. He removed the finish from commercial lines, then painstakingly applied red lead to give them density. He finished them with a Japanese dryer and paint pigment to give them color.

Syd Glasso and his last steelhead, on the Sol Duc River.

"Syd was an ingenious fellow and an inventive fellow," Dick Wentworth said. "He showed me the lines and let me help make them. I used to put the red lead on in my mother's kitchen. Most were 26 to 30 feet, and I'm sure they were over 10-weights. They had about a 10-foot butt, a 14-foot belly and the rest was tip. We weighted the line to fit the rod. We used Les Davis 25-pound monofilament for the running line. They would sink like a rock. The fly would be that far off the bottom," Dick said, spreading his hands about two feet apart.

To put Glasso's skill as a steelhead fly-fisherman in its proper perspective, it's important to remember the gear that was standard at the time and the way he went about presenting a fly to a steelhead. Glasso fished an Orvis Battenkill rod and Hardy reel for steelhead. Unlike many contemporary winter steelheaders, who use boats or two-handed rods to get their fly into position, Glasso waded deep and threw a long line. A large man, around six feet two inches tall, and an athlete, Glasso used his size and coordination to wade into positions other men avoided.

"Syd was a tremendous athlete," Wentworth said. "He was great at tennis and had played baseball. Lots of times he would cast over 100 feet, and we never used stripping baskets."

The End of the "Old Days"

It's hard to set a specific date for the end of the "old days" of Olympic Peninsula fly-fishing—that is, when there was less left to discover than had already been revealed. Trey Combs' first book, *The Steelhead Trout*, published in 1972, carried the first glimpse of Syd Glasso's Spey flies to a wider audience. But Dick Wentworth believes that fishing was in decline before that. "The glory days on the West End steelhead rivers were the 1950s," he told me recently. In Bill McMillan's recent *Historic Steelhead Abundance of North Coast and Puget Sound Streams*, he tells of a family that hiked into the upper Queets River for years for summer steelhead but gave it up in the 1950s because they thought it had become "too crowded." But compared to most of the Pacific Northwest Olympic rivers and lakes slumbered on for many years after Glasso became an icon.

You could make a case that the modern era of fly-fishing on the Olympic Peninsula began with the arrival of James Garrett. An employee of the Washington Department of Fisheries, Garrett created elegant and functional flies for steelhead, salmon and trout when he worked at the Dungeness, Elwha and Sol Duc hatcheries. Unlike Glasso, who worked alone or with a couple of like-minded anglers,

Dick Wentworth built this pirogue to float West End rivers during summer and fall low water.

Garrett became the president of the first Olympic Peninsula Federation of Fly Fishers chapter. It lobbied for and obtained a stretch of fly-only water on the upper Hoko during the winter. Garrett also taught fly-tying at Peninsula College in the 1980s, and later at Manuel Bernardo's Quality Fly Fishing Shop.

"The first meeting of the peninsula Federation of Fly Fishers chapter was in Jim's basement at the Dungeness Hatchery," J.D. Love said.

Even then, fishing remained pretty low key out here for a number of years. I routinely fished the Elwha, West End and Indian Island during the 1980s, and I was usually the only fly-fisher. I would see J.D. Love once in a while on the Sol Duc. He would be in his drift boat and I would be hiking or wading. We didn't know each other and simply nodded or waved, bound by the fact that we both had fly rods. As recently as the early 1990s, the middle Elwha, which frequently sees picket lines of fly rods today, was still lightly fished. I camped an entire summer on the Sol Duc in the middle 1980s, and I didn't see more than a half dozen fly-fishers.

Perhaps the most obvious point to set as the beginning of the modern era is when the peninsula got its first fly shop. Manuel Bernardo, who had done most of his previous fishing on Northern California steelhead and salmon rivers, opened Quality Fly-fishing shop in Port Angeles in the middle 1980s. Anyone who fished the Olympic Peninsula in those days knows what a relief it was to suddenly have a place where you could buy tippet and flies and tinsel without driving to Seattle or waiting for mail order. Mannie's shop also became a gathering place, where Olympic Peninsula fly-fishers from different towns encountered one another and exchanged information and the inevitable gossip.

"I didn't really get into winter steelhead on the fly until Mannie opened his shop," said Don Kaas. "I saw some of the more exotic materials and got into the Spey flies."

Quality Fly-fishing made everything a lot easier for Olympic Peninsula fly-fishers and it inspired an entire new crop of them. But it's hard to argue that the presence of a fly shop doesn't also signify the end of the old days in any remote area.

Part II

Section 1

Rain Forest Region

Fly originated by Syd Glasso; tied by John Alevras.

Sol Duc Spey

Hook: Partridge 1/0
Body: Rear 2/3, orange silk; front, seal substitute dubbing, hot-orange
Hackle: Schlappen, yellow, from second tinsel turn
Throat: Heron substitute (usually blue-eared pheasant) dyed black
Wing: 4 hackle tips, hot-orange

Left: ***Dave Steinbaugh swinging for spring steelhead on the Calawah.***

MAP D: Rain Forest Region

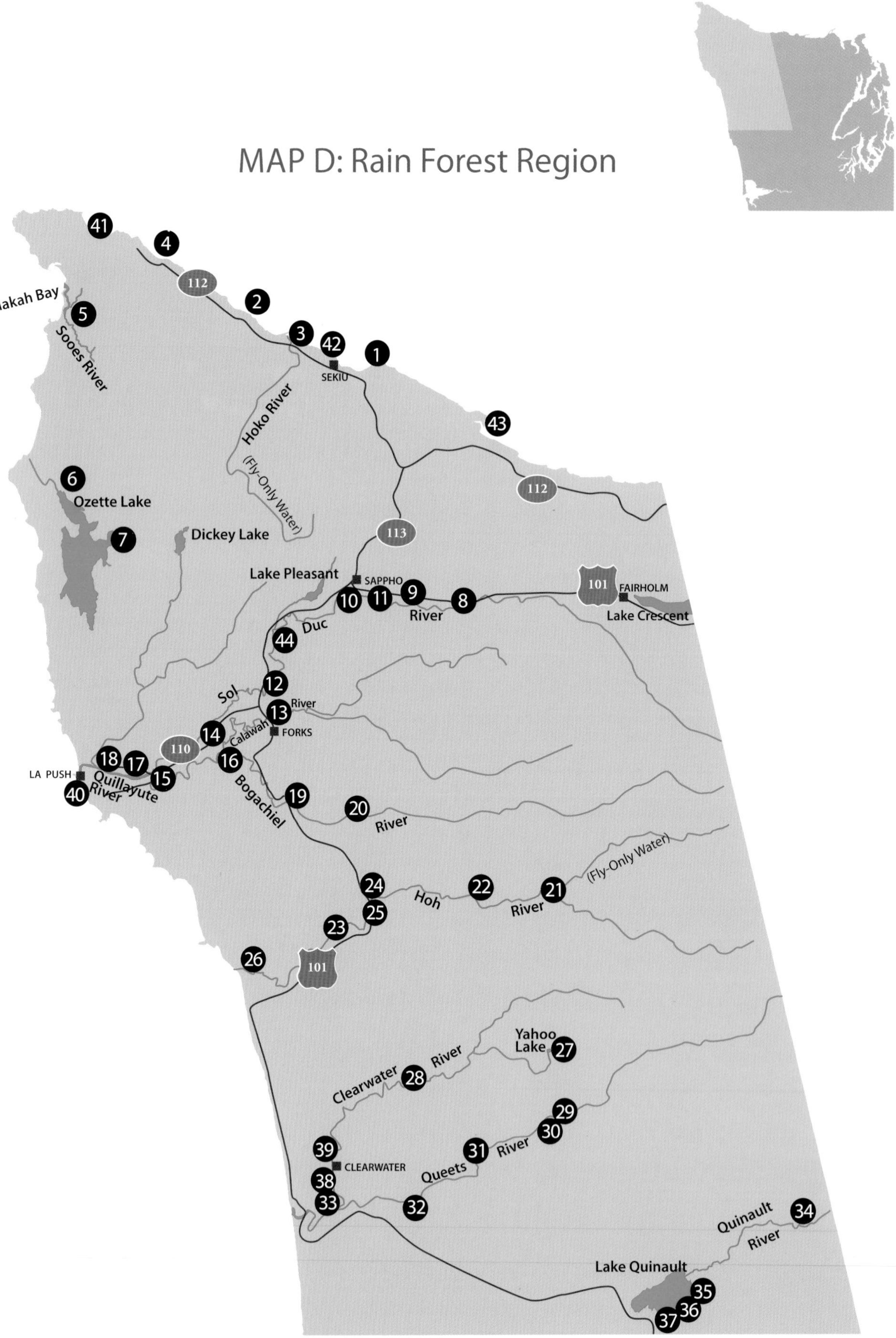

41
4
112
Makah Bay
5
Sooes River
2
3
42
1
SEKIU
Hoko River
(Fly-Only Water)
43
6
Ozette Lake
7
Dickey Lake
112
113
Lake Pleasant
SAPPHO
10
11
9
8
101
FAIRHOLM
Lake Crescent
Duc
River
44
12
Sol
River
13
Calawah
FORKS
14
110
16
18
17
15
LA PUSH
40
Quillayute
River
Bogachiel
19
20
River
24
Hoh
22
River
21
(Fly-Only Water)
25
23
26
101
Yahoo
Lake
27
Clearwater
28
River
29
30
31
River
Queets
39
CLEARWATER
38
33
32
Quinault
34
River
Lake Quinault
35
36
37

1. Clallam Bay Spit County Park beach access
2. Shipwreck Point Beach access
3. Hoko River State Park (proposed)
4. Snow Creek Resort
5. Sooes River (Tribal permit required on all Reservation land)
6. Ozette Beach Loop trailheads
7. Lost Resort
8. Riverside boat ramp (the ramp is very rough and the float is worse)
9. Hillstrom Road ramp (the "Bear Creek Drift" is even worse, beware!)
10. Sol Duc hatchery boat ramp
11. Sold Duc Sappho Salmon Hatchery
12. Whitcomb-Dimmel boat ramp
13. WDFW Calawah boat ramp (the lower Calawah is a dangerous float and should only be attempted by expert rowers who know the river.)
14. WDFW Goodman Mainline boat ramp (Sol Duc)
15. Wilson's boat ramp on the Bogachiel
16. Bogachiel Rearing Ponds boat ramp
17. Quillayute River Park access
18. Dickey River boat ramp (Olympic National Park)
19. Highway 101 boat ramp (Bogachiel)
20. WDFW Dowan's Creek access (no longer a ramp)
21. Olympic National Park Hoh River boat ramp
22. Morgan's Crossing boat ramp
23. Cottonwood boat ramp
24. Hoh Oxbow boat ramp
25. Allen's Bar boat ramp ($)
26. Barlows boat ramp ($)
27. Yahoo Lake (hike in 1/2 mile)
28. Coppermine Bottom boat ramp, rough 4X4 only.
29. Queets River trailhead (must ford river to reach trailhead; only safe at low water in late summer or fall)
30. Sams River boat ramp (rough)
31. Streator Crossing boat ramp
32. Hartzell Creed boat ramp
33. Queets Bridge boat ramp
34. Upper Quinault boat ramp
35. River take-out (behind Rain Forest Resort; must row across lake)
36. Falls Creek Campground ramp
37. Willaby Creek Campground ramp
38. Pioneer Memorial access ramp (very muddy)
39. Clearwater Bridge ramp
40. Marina & boat ramp
41. Marina & boat ramps
42. Marina & boat ramps
43. Pillar Point County Park and boat ramp
44. Maxfield Road boat ramp

Chapter Four

Sparkling Water and Spey Flies

Syd Glasso fishing the morning mists on the lower Sol Duc.

Springtime comes early on the Olympic Peninsula. With the exception of a few bitter mornings and an occasional burst of snow, winter on the West End could pass for spring in most areas of the country. It rains a lot, it's often windy, and the temperature regularly gets up into the forties, even low fifties. Midges and blue-winged olives are over the water on sunny afternoons, and by late February skunk cabbage blossoms brighten the alder bottoms. The main differences between winter and spring are the rain falls less frequently and with less intensity, and more hours of daylight increases the water temperature. The lower, clearer and warmer water make springtime the best time to catch a wild winter steelhead on a fly.

I spend most of my springtime steelheading on the Sol Duc. I've been fishing it a long time, and I know a lot of good fly-water on both the upper river, the area above the Salmon Hatchery at Sappho, and on the lower end, the portion below the old Rayonier Re-load off the Quilutete Airport Road. The Sol Duc is the first steelhead river I encounter when heading west from my home on the east side of the peninsula, and as long-time Port Angeles fly-fisherman, Don Kaas, says, "It's hard to pass by the Sol Duc." Syd Glasso took his 1959 *Field & Stream* record 18 3/4-pound steelhead from the Sol Duc on February 22, on the leading edge of an Olympic Peninsula spring.

One of my favorite pieces of water on the Sol Duc is a 100-yard-long run between two long steep rapids. It is only about a half mile from the road, but there isn't an obvious trail into it and you never see other anglers. I just follow an elk trail into the woods, over and around the tangles of moss-sheathed vine maple and old-growth Sitka spruce, toward the sound of the river. I always think I've overshot the drop to the river at some point, or that I am too far downstream. But I always come out right on the money. When the run is at the right level for fly-fishing, it is waist deep. A few large boulders and reef-like shelves break the flow, providing soft resting lies for the fish after the long uphill climb through the rapids.

I caught my last steelhead there, in mid-March. It hit the fly as it swung across the lower end of the run. A hen of about 12 pounds, it had pewter-flanks and a lipstick kiss of rose on its gill plates. I caught it on my Spey rod, with a

15-foot sink-tip, and one of Syd Glasso's patterns, the Sol Duc Dark. When Trey Combs asked Glasso which of his flies he recommended for the Quillayute System tributaries in spring, Glasso suggested the Orange Heron, Quillayute, and Sol Duc Dark. I didn't have any Orange Herons or any orange hackle tips for their wings, but I did have golden pheasant. I tied up a few of my rough versions of the Sol Duc Dark and the Quillayute, Glasso's protégé, Dick Wentworth's, excellent Spey fly.

With its strong run of wild fish and rich legacy of Glasso Spey flies, there may very well be no place in North America where the fish, the flies, the river conditions, and a river's fly-fishing heritage come together in such a compelling way as on the Sol Duc in spring. The Quillayute System produces more wild winter steelhead than any other river in the Pacific Northwest, including many in excess of 20 pounds and a few over 30, and the Sol Duc is by far the most productive component of the system. Syd Glasso's Spey flies were not simply the first North American Spey flies and the first for steelhead. His Sol Duc Series—Sol Duc, Sol Duc Spey and Sol Duc Dark—were created specifically for this river and its fish. For the handful of fly-fishers like Dick Wentworth and Pat Crane who knew him and fished with him, and those of us who have come subsequently, Glasso taught that a sense of beauty and grace in flies and tackle, a reverence for the fish, and affection for tradition were as important as killing fish.

As for the water conditions, the words Sol Duc are a corruption of the Quileute, "so is dak qu," which translates as "people who live near the clear, sparkling water." It is an apt description, because the Sol Duc runs clearer and cleans up faster than any other large West End river. This is partly a function of the fact that its headwaters on High Divide and Sol Duc Park are too low to support glaciers. In addition, more than 50 percent of the Sol Duc watershed lies within Olympic National Park, where logging and development are prohibited. The Sol Duc's limpid green water is also partly the result of geography. As the northern arm of the Quillayute System, the upper Sol Duc lies within a subtle but significant rain shadow behind Calawah Ridge and Hunger Mountain. It is frequently cloudy and misty on the upper river when it is raining hard on the Calawah and Bogachiel.

All of this comes together in spring. With longer days and warming sun, the water temperature rises into the mid 40s. That stimulates steelhead metabolisms, making them more likely to move to a fly. At the same time, the Sol Duc's water clarity lets you get away from the signal brightness of winter dressings, of patterns designed to catch the eye of a steelhead in high, turbid water. It probably isn't entirely a coincidence that drab flies and black flies become increasingly effective as insect activity increases in spring. I don't imagine adult winter steelhead eat many salmonfly nymphs crawling toward shore in spring or big October caddis larvae, but I don't believe they are oblivious to them either. Although Spey flies are usually described as suggesting shrimp or prawns, the leggy hackles of the dressings Glasso suggested for spring seem as "buggy" as they do shrimpy.

If the Sol Duc is the most dependably clear and low West End river in spring, its islands and pocket water and rock gardens present more presentation problems than the glacial rivers or even its sister river, the Bogachiel. The Sol Duc's in-river structure often prevents you from executing the long, slow, searching wet-fly swings that are easy on the Queets or Hoh. As a result, you tend to need heavier sink-tips, and you usually need to focus on small, discrete lies and set up swings with sharper downstream angles. The Sol Duc also has fewer and smaller gravel bars than the glacial rivers, and its tendency to remain in its channel allows trees and brush to grow close to the bank. This makes for difficult casting. Spey rods have ameliorated this to a great extent, but they haven't made the Sol Duc's rocks any easier to wade.

One way to cope with the complexity of flows is to dead-drift flies with a floating line. If you are good at it and know how to mend line and manipulate the rod skillfully, you can fish specific holding lies precisely. Combined with good water-reading skills or an intimate knowledge of the river, this can be truly deadly. In recent years, dead-drift nymphing has grown in popularity on the Sol Duc, and now most of the anglers who do it use strike indicators. Guides especially like the technique, because it lets them maneuver the boat to bring the line and fly into position rather than depending on the client's wading or casting skills.

This is Syd Glass water, though, and most veteran local fly-fishers save the nymphs and Glo Bugs for the creeks. On the Sol Duc, they stick with the wet-fly swing, and simply switch to the heavier sink-tips or weighted flies, sometimes even split shot, on the pocket water or boulder patches.

"I don't use anything but a dry line," Don Kaas said. "I've got a couple of sink-tips but I got tired of them. I just use a heavier hook or weighted fly in the rock gardens. I can fish places the gear guys avoid because they use too much gear."

Finally, the Sol Duc has a reputation for poor access, and many anglers think they need to book a float with a guide to have any chance at all. That's never a bad idea on the Sol Duc, because it's a tricky river to float, and a good guide will know the drifts that hold fish from the ones that look identical but never do. But anglers willing to study maps and poke around on foot will find plenty of accessible fly water. There is a lot of private property on the middle river, but timber companies, the Forest Service, and the State control most of the lower and upper river. You should never feel handicapped on the Sol Duc without a boat.

That's how Glasso fished it, after all. That's how Dick Wentworth still fishes it, and it's how many of the fly guides fish it on their days off.

It's all about finding water and fishing it intelligently.

Chapter Five

Hoh River Summer-Runs

Summer steelhead from a West End river.

The opportunity to catch a fish that you can take home and eat without guilt is appealing, even to some fly-fishers during these of days of diminished wild runs and restrictive harvest regulations. Almost all of us who grew up dragging trout, salmon and steelhead home now quickly release all of the wild fish we catch. But the allure of succulent red salmon steaks and roasts can become nearly irresistible when the target is hatchery salmon. And as the returns of hatchery silvers to West End rivers have increased in the wake of improving ocean conditions, a lot of fly-fishers have tried to quietly insinuate themselves among the bait and hardware anglers on the lower portions of the rivers in autumn.

I like to eat salmon too, but I have a hard time talking myself into fishing for anything other than summer steelhead if they are available. Summer steelhead are far less abundant on the Olympic Peninsula than winter fish, and significant wild populations only return to about a dozen streams, compared to more than 40 for winter steelhead. Typically ranging between 4 and 10 pounds, Olympic Peninsula summer fish are also smaller than wild winter steelhead, and they tend to swim and spawn higher in the watersheds. In Bill McMillan's recent report for the Wild Salmon Center, *Historic Steelhead Abundance in North Coast and Puget Sound Streams*, he recalled seeing two different home movies in the 1950s that showed trout anglers playing wild summer steelhead on Hoh Creek, only a few miles from Mount Olympus.

Summer steelhead were probably historically most abundant on the West End's large glacial systems, but they were commonly taken on the Elwha and Dungeness, the Duckabush, Humptulips, and, especially, the Quillayute System rivers. Even Morse Creek and the Pysht reportedly supported small runs of summer fish.

"I used to go up the North Fork of the Calawah near Shutz Pass in fall and get a limit of grouse in a few hours," Don Kaas said. "Then I'd catch a bunch of cutthroat. I got my first summer steelhead doing that. It hit a number 10 Humpy."

There aren't many wild Calawah summer steelhead left today, but it hosts a strong run of early-timed hatchery Skamania-stock fish between June and October. These fish are larger than the natives, ranging 8 to 15 pounds, and they provide fine sport on the lower six miles of the Bogachiel, which they must ascend to reach the Calawah, and, especially, around the Calawah's "ponds" at the Bogachiel Rearing Ponds. The Sol Duc receives a smaller plant of Skamania fish, and I have done quite well on them during early summer, often right after the June opener. The Wynoochee River has a large run of hatchery summer steelhead, although it is usually gunwhale to gunwhale with boats when fish are available, and there isn't much fly-fishing.

Of the glacial rivers, the Hoh is the best place to tangle with a summer steelhead on the fly today. In the 1940 edition of the Ben Paris *Washington Fishing Guide*, author Ken McCleod wrote enthusiastically about the Queets's summer fish, and Enos Bradner sang the praises of the upper Quinault in *Northwest Angling* (1950). But neither of these rivers is planted with summer steelhead and wild stocks have declined dramatically in recent years. Not that many more wild fish return to the Hoh, and it isn't planted with hatchery fish either, but "dip in" Skamania-stock hatchery steelhead from other rivers are common. In fact, summer snorkel surveys by Olympic National Park in recent years have identified more adipose-clipped steelhead on some reaches of the South Fork Hoh River than wild fish.

Actually, the best time to fish for "summer" steelhead on the Hoh is after Labor Day, when the previous winter's accumulation of snow has melted and cooling nighttime temperatures lock up the glaciers. The river is low enough to wade in places that you wouldn't dream of in winter, but it usually still has enough water to float drift boats. Unlike the Quillayute rivers, which can reach 70 degrees during early autumn droughts, the Hoh is nearly always cool enough for the fish to remain responsive. A floating line is often all you need, and the steelhead take traditional wet flies, as well as waking flies like Bill McMillan's Steelhead Caddis, skaters like Haig-Brown's Steelhead Bee, and the Lady Caroline on the greased line.

You can connect with Hoh summer-runs from tidewater to deep within the backcountry, but most are taken on the lower river, the section downstream of the Highway 101 bridge. However, the Hoh in Olympic National Park is one of my favorite places in the world, and the park's "fly only," catch-and-release water is one of my favorite places on the Hoh. The river opens on June 1 each year, and anglers may retain two hatchery steelhead. Extending approximately six miles, from the boat ramp near the park entrance upstream to just below the Hoh Campground, the fly water is paralleled loosely by the Upper Hoh River Road. The river is never exactly fishable from the road, but is usually less than a half-mile away. All of it is above the highest boat launch, so you will be spared the autumnal tune of people bouncing aluminum boats over rocks.

I once read a mystery in which a veteran detective told a rookie how he solved more cases than the other cops in the precinct: "You have to get off your ass and knock on doors." That's excellent advice for the Hoh fly-water. It has lots of washboard riffles, ankle-deep braids, and sandy flats where you aren't ever going to catch a steelhead. This discourages many anglers. But if you are persistent, you will find pools and creek mouths and seam lines below gravel bars where steelhead hold. They are usually spread out, and you have to hike to find them. Once you identify a few of these places, you can hike directly to them, fish hard, hike back out, and then drive upstream to your next sweet spot. That is my favorite way to fish any river, and it's really the only way to fish the Hoh fly-water.

Although it is one of my favorite things to do with a fly-rod, I sometimes worry about fishing for Hoh summer-runs. With so few wild fish left, it can seem rather self-indulgent even under catch-and-release regulations. There is some incidental mortality associated even with barbless hooks and the most carefully-handled steelhead, after all. It makes me uneasy when I release a fish that has fought hard and long. But then I think of the big, fin-clipped Skamania fish that are in the river with the Hoh natives. I catch nearly as many of them as I do wild fish. I kill every one I catch and eat it. I tell myself I'm performing a valuable service by preventing them from spawning with the natives.

So far, that rather slender reed of self justification keeps me heading back to the Hoh each October.

Chapter Six

Queets River Cutthroat

The cutthroat hit the Spruce fly hard, a sharp going away rap, and just kept going, up through the surface film and into the air. It jumped three times. Coastal cutthroat trout, *Oncorhynchus clarkii clarkii*, are different from most interior subspecies of cutthroat in that they frequently jump. Not always. Most of them are brawlers, favoring strong short surges, head shakes and surface thrashing. But this Queets River fish, only a dozen miles and a few tide changes from the Pacific Ocean, had about as much contact with the water as an egg-laying golden stonefly. When I finally brought it to hand, it was a bright 16-incher, and so thick I could barely cradle it in one hand.

Dick Wentworth took this nearly five-pound cutthroat on the Queets.

It was August, and the Queets was two days into transporting the first heavy rain since June back to the ocean. Although many people from outside the region imagine the West End in a perpetual state of drizzle and lamp-post-level clouds, the coast actually experiences something of a drought during late summer and early fall. Flows drop dramatically on the creeks, and by early September even the Quillayute System rivers have more exposed rock than water. I wrote a small piece for *Northwest Fly Fisherman* about fall cutthroat fishing in the Hoko River, and it came out during a record dry spell. I doubt anybody caught a cutthroat the entire time the issue was on the stands.

You don't have those problems on the Queets. The peninsula's second-largest watershed, the Queets is fed by glaciers on Mount Olympus and maintains good flows during the driest months of the year. That lets schools of sea-run cutthroat enter from the Pacific Ocean as early as mid-summer. Although they spawn higher than any other species of anadromous fish except native char, they are easiest to catch on the lower portions of rivers, where the gradient is flatter and before they have dispersed. They take up stations around root wads and snags, in dark pools, and along the soft edges of the main channel. Ranging from slender 8-inchers to heavy fish pushing the 20-inch mark, they will hit everything from traditional wet flies, like the Spruce and Knutson's Spiders, to hair-winged dry flies, and tiny *Baetis* emergers.

"Syd and I used to fish the Queets," Dick Wentworth recalled. "I caught a 19 3/4-inch cutthroat there. It must have weighed nearly five pounds."

Sea-run cutthroat are available on virtually every West End creek and river, and every one of them is a wild fish. Their numbers certainly aren't as high as they were when Dick fished them with Syd Glasso, but there are enough around that you can usually find fish. Even better, sea-runs don't have much of a following among gear and bait anglers these days, so fly-fishers usually have the good cutthroat water to themselves. Unlike the sea-runs of the northeastern Olympic Rain Shadow, which tend to remain in salt water until winter rains bring up the water level in the creeks, some migratory cutts enter the large West End rivers by midsummer, or even earlier.

"There were big cutthroat in the Queets and Humptulips in spring," Wentworth said. "They had blue back and silver bodies. They would spawn and the holdovers were the ones we called 'yellow-bellies.' The big push of fall sea-runs came with the first high water in late September."

I don't know if Roderick Haig-Brown ever fished the Queets, but he made several trips to the nearby Quinault River, and wrote about it in *Sports Illustrated* in April of 1958. He described a September trip on the lower river with Jonah Cole, a Quinault Indian guide. They caught trout to 16 inches, but Cole told Haig-Brown that cutthroat fishing was best in July. "Apparently there is a good run of fish in from the sea at that time and probably fair numbers of fish drop back from the lake as well," he wrote. "It must be a feeding movement and presumably reflects some special activity of crayfish, salmon fry or insects, perhaps all three. . . In most streams the Coast cutthroat run begins to show in late July and early August and builds from there."

Queets River sea-runs have several things going for them that make them particularly attractive to fly-fishers. Other than its lower six miles, which flow through the Quinault Indian Reservation, the Queets is entirely within the boundaries of Olympic National Park, and is managed as a natural area. That means there are no houses, no clear-cuts and no "no trespassing" signs. There are also no summer salmon seasons on the Queets and not very many summer steelhead. That means you will be pretty much alone until the first fall chinook and hatchery coho arrive in September. The park manages Queets trout under catch-and-release regulations, which tends to send anglers who want to eat cutthroat to those portions of rivers located outside the National Park.

"The primary management objectives at Olympic National Park are to preserve and restore native fishes and their habitats and to provide high quality and diverse recreational fishing opportunities for the enjoyment of park visitors," explained Sam Brenkman, ONP fisheries biologist. "We also routinely consult with the State and Treaty Tribes on the annual regulations. But we emphasize catch-and-release of wild fish and harvest of hatchery and non-native fish."

Finally, Haig-Brown took most of his Quinault River cutts on his coho fry pattern, the Silver Brown. I thought of that when Dick Wentworth first showed me his cutthroat fly box. I don't know what I was expecting, perhaps some small Orange Herons or his Quillayute. Instead, I beheld rows of small, beautifully dressed Silver Browns, Silver Ladys, Lady Carolines, Silver Doctors and Royal Coachmen streamers and bucktails. There were also a number of elegant sculpin patterns. Not that many anglers fish these dressings today, but they are all excellent flies for West End cutthroat in general and Queets River cutthroat in particular.

"I got a lot of my cutthroat patterns from reading Haig-Brown," Dick said. "I bought a copy of the *Western Angler* in Port Angeles when I was 15. I was supposed to buy a present with the money, and my mother got mad at me for buying the book." Dick has taken West End cutthroat on the Haig-Brown dressings and traditional feather wings for 50 years. "It's the same kind of country and the same fish as Vancouver Island." As for the sculpin patterns, Dick says his uncle Mickey Merchant pointed him in that direction. "He told me, 'If you want to catch big cutthroat, find a fly that imitates a bullhead.'"

Rivers

Western Strait of Juan de Fuca

Highway 112 "Cedar Creeks": These small to medium-sized streams rise up on the ridges that extend between Lake Crescent and Neah Bay and drop quickly over logged-over land to pocket estuaries and small bays. They carry a tannin stain from cedars year-round, and are characterized by snags and sweepers, pocket pools, cuttbanks and short riffles. They are very low during summer and provide little fishing until the first significant fall rains. They originally supported strong wild runs of coho and chum salmon, sea-run cutthroat, winter steelhead and several hosted fall chinook. Today, there are no salmon seasons on any of these streams, and most angling targets hatchery winter steelhead in December and January. Sea-run cutthroat return between September and November.

Deep Creek: Although the WDFW no longer plants it with hatchery fish, the creek is open to steelhead fishing in winter. The agency apparently thinks it gets enough strays to warrant a fishery. It makes more sense to avoid Deep Creek entirely and give its few remaining wild fish a break.

West/East Twin: These two creeks flow into the strait about a mile apart. They don't offer a lot of fishing opportunity, but the lower pools can hold sea-run cutthroat in fall.

Pysht River: The Pysht is the second-largest river flowing into the western strait, and historically it and the Hoko were the western strait's most productive rivers. Most fishing today is focused on winter steelhead, along with some sea-run cutthroat angling in autumn if there is enough water. The Merrill-Ring Tree Farm (360-452-2367) owns nearly all the land on the lower river, and charges an annual access fee.

Clallam River: Anglers who don't mind hiking around gated log roads and bucking brush can find some winter steelhead on the upper reaches of the Clallam River. It flows into the strait within the community of Clallam Bay, behind mile-long Clallam Bay Spit. The river's mouth is frequently blocked by sand bars, trapping outmigrating juvenile salmon and trout in the estuary. The strait side of the spit can be worth a try when staging salmon or cutthroat are waiting for increased river flow to cut an opening in the spit. The Clallam Bay Spit County Park provides access (Map D1).

Hoko River: With 25 miles of mainstem, the Hoko (Map D3) is the largest river flowing into the western strait. Although you may see everything from fall chinook to coho to chum, the only legal fisheries are for cutthroat and winter steelhead. The Hoko is "fly only" and catch-and-release during September and October, and you can fish for sea-runs in virtual solitude if there has been enough rain to bring the fish in. The Hoko's winter steelhead "fly only" water, the first fly-only water for winter steelhead in Washington, is located between the upper Hoko River Bridge and Ellis Creek. Unfortunately, it is all on timber company land and is gated (if the gates are open don't assume they'll remain that way until you want to leave). Even if you hike or bicycle beyond the gates, the log roads only touch the river occasionally. The Hoko has the Strait of Juan de Fuca's strongest run of wild winter steelhead.

Sekiu River: The Sekiu splits into a north and south fork five miles above Highway 112. Winter steelhead, which are open through February to the forks, and a small run of sea-runs are the attraction.

Pacific Ocean

Sooes River: The Sooes River, which flows into the Pacific Ocean at Makah Bay on the Makah Indian Reservation, provides unique fishing in a remote setting for chinook, coho, sea-run cutthroat and winter steelhead. Most effort is concentrated downstream of the Makah National Fish Hatchery. Tribal fishing permits, which can be purchased locally, are required on all reservation waters, including the nearby Waatch River and salt water beaches.

Ozette River: The outlet of Lake Ozette, the Ozette River only flows about five miles before merging with the ocean north of Cape Alava. There is little fishing near the lake, and the only way to reach the mouth is by hiking the Ozette Loop Trail, then tramping the coast for two miles to the estuary. Sockeye salmon were the river's most famous stock but are now listed as threatened under the ESA. There is very little fishing of any kind in the Ozette, and no salmon seasons.

Quillayute System

Draining 750 square miles, the Quillayute System is the Olympics' largest watershed if you exclude the Chehalis River, which isn't located entirely on the peninsula. In addition to the strongest wild winter steelhead stocks in the Pacific Northwest, it hosts every salmon species native to North American, including sockeye, all three races of chinook, summer steelhead, cutthroat and headwater char. You can fish for all of them except the char, which are protected under the ESA everywhere on the peninsula. The Quillayute tributaries—the Sol Duc, Bogachiel, Calawah and Dickey—are not glacial and, consequently, run clearer and stay in shape longer than the rain forest systems. They are a good bet when the Hoh and Queets are blown out, but can be tough during summer low water.

Quillayute: The Quillayute River mainstem is only six miles long. It is big, low gradient, and effected by tides in its lower reaches. In his 1950 classic *Northwest Angling*, Enos Bradner described it this way: "From early December until late in April steelhead surge into the broad slow reaches and sparkling riffles of the Quillayute in one fine run after the other." That is still true, and fly-fishers also have a shot at salmon from March through November and cutthroat from midsummer through autumn. The best access is at the Clallam County Quillayute River Park (Map D17), off the Mora Road a couple miles west of Lyendecker. Boats can launch at Lyendecker County Park and take out at the Dickey River ramp (Map D18).

Dickey: It looks like a creek, but the Dickey's mainstem and east, middle and west forks drain an immense watershed. With a nearly uniformly low gradient, it is a vast watery maze of sloughs and side channels, ponds and wetlands. That is perfect coho habitat, and the Dickey was one of Washington's most productive coho systems. In recent years, all species have declined, but winter steelhead, sea-run cutthroat and fall coho provide interesting fishing. Access to the mainstem is from the Mina Smith Road, while you need to explore timber roads, many of which are gated, to reach the forks. "The Dickey River cutthroat ate a lot of crayfish," said Dick Wentworth, whose ancestors homestead was close to the river. "They had real dark bodies and red flesh."

Bogachiel: The Bogachiel offers fly-fishers everything from hike-in cutthroat in Olympic National Park to chinook and coho salmon on the lower river to the peninsula's most crowded winter steelhead fishing. Its most popular boat launch (Map D16) is located at the Bogachiel Rearing Ponds in Forks, and winter and summer steelheaders drift down to Wilson's Boat Ramp or Lyendecker, at the Bogey's confluence with the Sol Duc. Every hatchery summer steelhead that eventually returns to the Calawah's "ponds" must first negotiate the lower six miles of the Bogachiel, and the lower river is a popular midsummer and early fall destination. Excellent sea-run cutthroat fishing is available downstream of the hatchery from late summer through October. The Bogachiel is the easiest Quillayute tributary to float, and a launch under the U.S. 101 Bridge (Map D19) lets you fish the water above the hatchery. The Bogachiel Trail (Map D20) begins at the end of Undie Road and Forest Road 2932 and extends 30 miles to Seven Lakes Basin.

Calawah: The Calawah, which means "in between," is a tributary of the Bogachiel, and flows between it and the Sol Duc. It is smaller and more intimate than its sister rivers and is characterized by shelves, dark pools and rocky flats. Its mouth is located near the Bogachiel Rearing Pond and attracts huge crowds of winter steelheaders during December and early January. The "ponds," the walk-in area near the rearing pond, are also popular with all types of anglers when hatchery summer-runs return between July and October. Fewer fish and fewer anglers venture above Highway 101, but the upper mainstem and north and south forks contain some sea-run and resident cutthroat. Although a new WDFW ramp near Forks provides boat access to the water between Highway 101 and the Bogachiel Rearing Ponds, the lower Calawah is a dangerous float and should only be attempted by expert rowers who know the river (Map D13).

Sol Duc: Syd Glasso loved the lower end of the Sol Duc, the reach within a mile or so of Lyendecker, but anadromous fish swim all the way to Sol Duc Falls, at River Mile 65. The lower river is open virtually year-round, with winter steelhead available through spring, spring chinook beginning in February, and sea-runs, salmon and summer steelhead in summer and fall. The Sol Duc receives a small run of sockeye in early to midsummer, and a stock of "summer coho" in August and September. Much of the lower Sol Duc, the reach from the mouth upstream to the WDFW boat ramp on the Goodman Mainline (Map D14), is timber company land, and you can access it from the Mora Road, Quillayute Airport Road and Goodman Mainline. The middle river continues upstream to the salmon hatchery at Sappho (Map D11), and contains a mix of private property and timberlands. Access to the upper river is available at the hatchery (Map D10), Tumbling Rapids Campground, Bear Creek Campground (Map D9), Klahowya Campground and along the Olympic Hot Springs Road in the park. The floats from Riverside (Map D8) to Hillstrom Road and, especially, Hillstrom Road to the hatchery are dangerous, but the middle and lower rivers are more manageable. Ramps at the hatchery, Maxfield Road and Whitcomb-Dimmel Road provide boat access to the middle river (Map D12).

Glacial Rain Forest Rivers

With their long gravel bars, enormous log jams and glacial green tint, the rivers of the rain forest valleys are as different from the Quillayute System rivers as they are from the rain shadow streams to the east. Bull trout, summer steelhead, and spring chinook are more common in these big, cold rivers than in other peninsula streams. You will enjoy fewer fishing days, because rainfall and glacial melt knock them out of shape for days at a time, but they are better bets when the Quillayute rivers are low and warm in summer, or low and cold in winter. It is nearly always possible to float the lower ends of the glacial rivers.

Hoh River: Sport anglers take more winter and summer steelhead, chinook and coho from the Hoh than the other rain forest rivers combined. With the exception of a brief interlude between the end of the winter steelhead season on April 15 and the opening of chinook salmon on May 16, the Hoh is also always open. Winter steelhead attract the most attention. Hatchery fish planted by the Hoh Tribe are abundant below Highway 101 during early winter, while its wild run is available from the mouth into the national park by mid-February. The Hoh provides spring/summer chinook fishing after mid-May, although not many are taken on flies. Fall kings and coho are more abundant, and the action is concentrated below the highway. The best summer steelheading occurs after summertime run-off is over and the first cool nights lock up the glaciers. Sea-runs are in the river at the same time as the summer-runs, and in October it isn't unusual to take cutthroat, steelhead and coho on the same day. Of the three glacial systems, the Hoh is the easiest for visitors to negotiate on their own. From its mouth, which flows between the Hoh Indian Reservation and Olympic National Park's coastal strip, to the ONP boundary upstream, there is little water that you can't access by foot and none that a good oarsman can't float. The 6-mile reach in ONP between the boat ramp and one-quarter mile downstream of the Hoh Campground is fly-only and catch-and-release year round.

Goodman Creek: Goodman Creek is a small independent drainage, flowing into the ocean between the Quillayute and Hoh. It is only open to winter steelhead and trout. Old maps show a trail from Highway 101 to the mouth. "A new trail leaves Olympic Highway about three miles south of Bogachiel River tourist camp," the 1940 Ben Paris fishing pamphlet said, "following down Goodman Creek to its mouth at the ocean." Unfortunately, only vestiges of the trail exist today, and the only practical way to fish the creek is from the Goodman Mainline (Rayonier 3000), the log road between the Oil City Road and Mora Road. Most anglers fish near the bridge, but more ambitious folks can bushwack up and downstream. It's always a good idea to stop in Forks and make sure the mainline is passable.

Mosquito Creek: Mosquito Creek is a sea-run and winter steelhead stream frequented by only a handful of anglers. It is usually too low in summer for sea-runs, but you can have a fine day after a decent fall rain. It is also a good spot for nymphs and Glo Bugs during the winter. The Goodman Mainline and spurs provide access.

Kalaloch Creek: A snaggy, cedar-stained creek that flows into the ocean within sight of Kalaloch Lodge, Kalaloch Creek provides limited sea-run cutthroat and winter steelhead fishing. Its lower reaches are within ONP's coastal strip, and are catch-and-release (except for hatchery steelhead, which aren't planted) with single, barbless-hook artificial lures and flies. The state land upstream is managed under selective fishery regulations. Both reaches open in June and close at the end of February.

Queets River: Draining 445 square miles and with more than 50 miles of mainstem, the Queets is the peninsula's second-largest watershed. It flows entirely through Olympic National Park until it enters the Quinault Indian Reservation, six miles upstream of the ocean. Best known as a winter steelhead river, its wild-run size has ranged from 16,000 in 1971-72 to 8,000 in 1993-94. Enos Bradner dedicated more words to the Queets in *Northwest Angling* than any other peninsula river outside the Quillayute System. It has winter and summer steelhead, spring, summer and fall chinook (only fall kings have been open in recent years), and a strong run of hatchery coho. Wild summer steelhead numbers have been extremely low in recent years, but sea-run cutthroat seem abundant and widespread. The only access is from the Queets River Road—a rough, muddy gravel road that extends 13 miles from Highway 101 to the Queets Campground. When it is open, the road provides boating fly-fishers access to the river's three ramps and to turn-outs from which anglers can hike to the river, which is seldom more than a half mile distant. However, the road is subject to slides and wash-outs, and currently a massive wash-out at Matheny Creek prevents all access above RM 6.5. The park has announced that it will open an alternate route to the upper Queets via DNR and Forest Service by early 2008. The Queets River Trail (Map D29) begins on the north side of the river, across from the campground, which means that you have to ford the river to reach it. This is only safe during the low water of late summer and early autumn. The Queets goes out even quicker than the Hoh and experiences a river-changing flood every decade or so.

Salmon River: The Quinault Tribe's hatchery on Salmon River, a lower Queets tributary, pumps winter steelhead, chinook and an early-timed (September) stock of coho into the river. In recent years, the Salmon has accounted for as many, if not more, steelhead than the mainstem. You need a tribal guide to fish the reservation portion of the Salmon, but not the park water downstream or the state water above the reservation. The Salmon is creek-sized, and dead-drifting flies is a good strategy.

Clearwater River: The Clearwater flows into the Queets just inside the Quinault Indian Reservation Boundary. It is the Queets' largest tributary, and its 153-square-mile watershed is as large as the Bogachiel's. As its name suggests, it is a clean-running stream, the result of headwaters on non-glacial Owl Mountain. Most fly-fishing targets cutthroat in fall, coho in October and November, and steelhead in winter and early spring. Although it has more than 35 miles of mainstem—and major tributaries such as Sollecks, Stequahello and Snahapish rivers—most angling is concentrated below its junction with the Snahapish River. The Clearwater Mainline, the major log road between the Hoh and Queets, provides access to the lower river. The ramp at the DNR's Coppermine Bottom Campground is frequently mud-covered and is only suitable for beefy 4X4 vehicles. The next ramp downstream is beneath the Clearwater Bridge. The lowest ramp outside the Quinault Indian Reservation is at the DNR's Pioneer Memorial Access near the hamlet of Clearwater. The road into it is also frequently a sea of mud. Although maps show a number of rapids, the Clearwater is no harder to float than other moderately difficult West End streams. Above the Snahapish, the river jogs east and the Clearwater 3000 road provides access to the Upper Clearwater Campground. The upper Clearwater is now within the DNR's Clearwater Corridor Natural Reserve Conservation Area, where logging and other development are prohibited. The lower Snahapish River is also protected in an NRCA.

Quinault River: The Quinault is divided into an upper and lower river separated by Lake Quinault. The 35 miles of river below the lake are entirely within the Quinault Indian Reservation, and you must hire a tribal guide to fish it. The Quinault National Fish Hatchery and Quinault Tribe release hundreds of thousands of winter steelhead, chinook, chum and coho salmon annually, and you probably stand a better chance of taking these species on the lower Quinault than any other Olympic River.

The lower Quinault is also known for excellent summertime sea-run cutthroat fishing, and Roderick Haig-Brown and Supreme Court Justice William O. Douglas fished it from dugout canoes in the 1950s. Tribal guides know the river intimately but make sure you mention you want to fly-fish before booking a trip. The lower end of the upper river flows through Olympic National Forest and the upper mainstem and forks are within Olympic National Park. Ranging from Mount Anderson on the east to Low Divide on the north and Skyline Ridge on the west, the Quinault's east and west forks drain an immense basin. However, most of it is leeward of the ocean, and the upper river cleans up more quickly than the Hoh or Queets and is often very clear in spring.

Winter steelhead are the main show on the upper mainstem, and although it turns out far fewer fish than the reservation water most are wild and some are quite large. A couple of years ago, an angler caught and released an estimated 35-pound winter steelhead (46 inches). Private property restricts foot access, and most winter angling is done from boats. The upper Quinault has an abundance of log jams and braids, and boaters should scout bends and exercise caution. Boats launch (Map D34) at the bridge and take out at the Rain Forest Inn (Map D35) on the lake. Afternoon thermals can kick up a chop on the lake, and the mile-long row to the haul-out is often the most difficult part of the day. Trails follow both forks deep into Olympic National Park wilderness, but there aren't a lot of trout and it is illegal to pursue native char. Summer steelhead once supported popular backcountry fisheries, but there are few today. Mountain whitefish are relatively abundant and can provide exciting catch-and-release angling with small nymphs.

Lakes

Lake Ozette (Ozette): More than eight miles long, with an average width of two miles, Lake Ozette is the third-largest natural lake in Washington. It contains many inlets, and its outlet, the Ozette River, drains to the Pacific Ocean. Everything from sockeye to winter steelhead to coho migrates through the lake to spawning tributaries, and imbeciles have planted perch and largemouth bass. The only significant fly-fishing is for cutthroat trout, and biologists believe the lake contains adfluvial fish and sea-runs. Ozette is entirely within ONP, and fishing is restricted to catch-and-release (for trout) and artificial lures with single, barbless hooks. Recent research has shown that larger cutthroat feed heavily on outmigrating sockeye fry in spring and early summer. Camping is available at the park's Ozette Campground and the Lost Resort (Map D7) (360-963-2899), and ramps are available on Swan Bay and in the park. There is little bank fishing, and Ozette is no place for float tubes or paddle boats, because coastal wind and rain can make this big shallow lake treacherous.

Beaver Lake (Sol Duc): Located three miles north of Sappho on the Burnt Mountain Road, Beaver Lake covers 36 acres but is surrounded by a much larger swamp. This is how E.B. Webster described Beaver Lake in his 1922 volume *Fishing in the Olympics*, ". . . Beaver Lake, a mile long widening of Beaver Creek, probably has more (cutthroat) to the square foot than are to be found elsewhere in the Northwest." It still has a lot of small cutts, but perch and other non-native fish are also now in the lake. It is a fine place to take a youngster or beginning fly-fisher. Rough boat launches.

Lake Pleasant (Sol Duc): Lake Pleasant is two miles long and covers 486 acres. Sockeye salmon, which swim up Lake Creek from the Sol Duc, still return to the lake but are off limits, although you can keep kokanee between 8 and 20 inches. Cutthroat, some in excess of two pounds, were taken until quite recently, but fishing has fallen off dramatically. "I think they need to do a study to see what's going on up there," Dick Wentworth said. A boat ramp is located at the community park in Beaver.

Mink Lake (Sol Duc): Only 2.4 miles from the Sol Duc Hot Springs parking lot and with an elevation gain of 1,400 feet, 10-acre Mink Lake (3,080 feet) is an excellent day-hiking destination from late spring through fall. It is surrounded by montane zone forest and has an abundance of submerged vegetation. Brook trout are self-sustaining and reach 15 inches, although most are smaller. It has scuds and crayfish.

Wentworth Lake (Dickey): Named for Dick Wentworth's family, whose homestead was a few miles to the south, 54-acre Wentworth Lake drains to the Middle Fork of the Dickey. Cutthroat are native, but it has been poisoned and replanted several times, and now has rainbows. It was easy to reach before the bridge on the Mina Smith Road collapsed, but now you must approach it from the Gunderson side (off Highway 101) on log roads. The ramp is in bad shape, and car-toppers are your best bet.

Dickey Lake (Dickey): The largest lake in the Quillayute System, covering 527 acres, Dickey Lake receives very light fishing pressure. Part of the reason is its location at the end of number of log roads, which may be gated at times, but the fishing isn't that good either and there are a lot of squawfish. It originally supported fine runs of cutthroat, coho and sockeye, which the Quileute Indians caught in woven traps.

Yahoo Lake (Queets/Clearwater): Unless you are obsessed with solitude, the rewards of Yahoo Lake probably aren't worth the effort. Located at 2,350 feet, in the upper reaches of the Stequaleho Creek basin, this 3-acre lake contains cutthroat and the State plants it with fry. To reach it, (Map D27) you must first drive up the Clearwater Mainline to the C3000 road, then turn onto the C3100 road and follow it to the gate, a half-mile from the lake. The DNR maintains a walk-in campground, but it is used mostly by elk hunters.

Irely Lake (North Fork Quinault): Less than a mile from the North Fork Campground on the Big Creek Trail, Irely Lake's size ranges from four to more than 20 acres depending on rainfall. Its low elevation (550 feet) means that you can reach it any time it is open (late April through October). It contains wild cutthroat, and ONP manages it with catch-and-release, no bait, and single barbless hook regulations. The trailhead is located near the end of the North Shore Road.

Lake Quinault: Three miles long and with an average depth of 133 feet and maximum depth of 240 feet, Lake Quinault is the Olympic Peninsula's third-largest natural lake. Lake Quinault sockeye have been legendary for more than a century, and the Quinault Indian Tribe still harvest and market them. The tribe controls all fishing on the lake and requires a permit, which can be obtained at the Quinault Mercantile (360-288-2620) and other locations. There is no fishing for sockeye or other salmon, but it turns out some hefty rainbow and cutthroat and not that many fly-anglers pursue them. With all of the migrating juvenile salmon and steelhead, this is an excellent place to fish fry and smolt patterns. The lake has several resorts and three Forest Service campgrounds. Boat launches are available at the Falls Creek (Map D36) and Willaby campgrounds (Map D37). Lake Quinault can become quite windy in the afternoon and during storms.

Section 2
Rain-Shadow Area

Fly originated by James Garrett; tied by Curtis Reed.

Orange and Black Olympic Stonefly

Hook: Partridge, 4 and 6
Tail: Peacock primary feather dyed black
Tag: Floss, fluorescent flame
Underbody: Polypropylene, black and black chenille
Overbody: Chenille, black and hot-orange yarn woven
Caseback: Polypropylene, black and black webby hackle
Head: Floss, black

MAP A: Rain Shadow Area

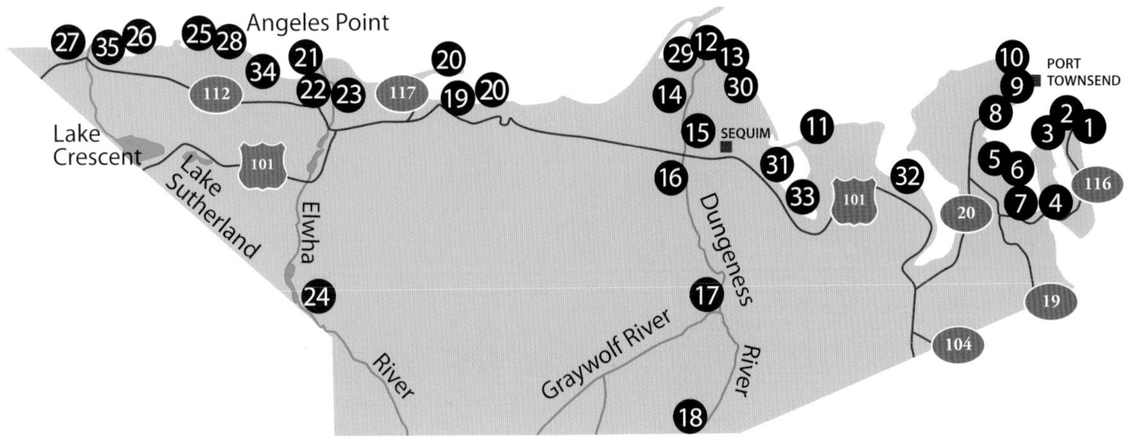

1. Marrowstone Point
2. Boat ramp
3. Boat ramp
4. Indian Island beach access
5. Mouth of Chimacum Creek
6. Chimacum Creek beach access
7. Lower Hadlock boat ramp (This provides boat access to Port Townsend Bay and Chimacum Creek mouth from lower Port Hadlock)
8. Port of Port Townsend boat ramp (Located within Port Townsend, this ramp makes for an easy run to Admiralty Inlet and Port Townsend Bay)
9. Fort Worden boat ramp
10. Point Wilson
11. Panorama Vista County beach access
12. Port of Port Angeles boat ramp
13. Old Dungeness School access
14. Wheeler River County Park beach access
15. Railroad Bridge Park access
16. Three Rivers County Park access
17. Lower Graywolf River trailhead
18. Upper Dungeness River trailhead
19. Port Angeles Boat Haven ramp
20. Waterfront trail access
21. Place Road access to mouth of Elwha
22. Sisson access
23. WDFW Elwha rearing channel access
24. Elwha River trailhead
25. Crescent Beach Resort access $
26. Whiskey Creek Beach Resort access $
27. Murdock Creek beach access
28. Salt Creek Recreation Area
29. Cline Spit Ramp
30. Marilyn Nelson County Park Access
31. John Wayne Marina and ramp
32. Gardiner boat ramp
33. Sequim Bay State Park & Ramp (on west shore)
34. Fresh water Bay Ramp
35. Lyre River Campground access

Chapter Seven

The Periwinkle Hatch

It's kind of tricky writing about the Elwha these days. The two dams that have blocked migratory fish from all but the lowest 4.9 miles of the river for the last 80 years are scheduled to begin coming down by 2012. That will provide salmon, steelhead and trout access to the 83 percent of the watershed that lies above the lower dam. Most biologists believe Elwha dam removal holds more promise of fish restoration than any other project in the Pacific Northwest. But biologists also concede the resident rainbow trout population, which has provided the only sport fishing on the middle and upper river since the dams were built, will be most likely be reduced. The State, tribes and national park have also agreed to close the Elwha for five years after the dams are removed to allow anadromous fish to re-colonize the river.

Rock hopping on the Middle Elwha during late summer.

So do I emphasize the trout that you can fish for today, arguably the best resident rainbow trout fishing in western Washington? After all, you won't be able to fish for them in a few years, and the fishery may never again be as good as it is now. Or should I write about future fly-fishing for salmon and steelhead? I am confident the middle and upper Elwha will eventually support strong runs of chinook and coho and summer and winter steelhead, but there are no guarantees that the restoration will unfold as planned. The river remains open to fishing inside Olympic National Park from June 1 through October 31.

Well, I'm going to take the craven route and narrow my focus to one species that is already in the river, *Oncorhynchus mykiss,* and I'm going to cover my bets by writing about both resident rainbows and summer steelhead. Rainbows are already abundant above the lower dam, and I believe steelhead have arguably the best chance of quickly re-colonizing the middle and upper river.

In 1907, the Seattle-based hiking and climbing organization, the Mountaineers, trekked up the Elwha to Mount Olympus for its summer outing. Aeshel Curtis, brother of renowned American Indian photographer Samuel Curtis, served as the group's photographer. On August 1, he took a photograph of a young expedition member, Elinor Chittenden, holding a summer steelhead and a fly rod. There was no notation as to who actually caught the fish (the rod has no reel attached) or where it was taken. However, Olympic Peninsula historian and author, Harriet Fish, researched the sequence of Curtis photos and found that the Chittenden shot was taken deep in the Olympics, within sight of Mount Seattle and glaciers. My wife is 5 foot 3, and a distance on her comparable to the length of the steelhead in the photo is just shy of 30 inches.

Dick Goin has fished the Elwha since the 1930s. "A really big day on summer runs was two fish," he said. "They were always the frosting. They were short and stumpy with deep bodies and little heads. They would jump 20 times. The kings spawned in those days between 5 and 10 October. They were very common around the bridge. Everything else was behind them. There was a sort of pecking order. There would be trout and sea-run cutthroat and Dollies, anadromous and resident, and mixed in with them were the summer steelhead and half-pounders. The first fish you hooked would always be an adult summer steelhead."

The Elwha Dams are scheduled to begin coming down by 2012.

A lot of factors will play into whether fish like those re-establish themselves above the dams, but habitat won't be a problem. More than 70 percent of the watershed lies above Lake Mills (actually reservoir), within Olympic National Park wilderness. Moreover, unlike many Olympic Peninsula rivers, where impassible waterfalls block access to large areas of the upper watershed, the most distant reaches of the upper Elwha are navigable to strong swimmers and jumpers like steelhead, chinook and coho. Even the middle river, the reach between the Glines Canyon (upper) dam and Lake Aldwell, is in good shape compared to many western Washington rivers.

On the Olympic Peninsula, as on most coastal areas, anadromous rainbows, that is, steelhead are the norm, and resident trout are spread pretty thinly. Individual fish, as a rule, don't get very big. But from the earliest reports, the Elwha apparently turned out hefty rainbows. "Here he grows to a truly immense size," E. B. Webster wrote in his 1922 volume, *Fishing in the Olympics*, "specimens eighteen and twenty inches in length being if not common, at least sufficiently so that one would never think of packing them very far for the pleasure of exhibiting them to his friends." Initially, I was somewhat skeptical of this, figuring these fish were steelhead, maybe half-pounders, that had been trapped above the dams or were mis-identified Dollies or bull trout. But Dick Goin has fished the Elwha since the 1930s and knows what he is talking about. He says it had large resident rainbows and a rainbow/cutthroat hybrid.

"Resident trout were so rich, even in the presence of anadromy," he told me. "There were rainbow and hybrid rainbow/cutthroat to three and four pounds, some six pounds. There were a lot more in the lower river than the upper. 'Four-stripers' is what we called the natural hybrid. I don't think there are any left. They were big enough to get into nets. I loved to fish for them, loved to fish the canyon. They were very responsive to the dry fly."

According to Dick, there was a lot for Elwha trout to eat before the dams gradually destroyed the processes that maintained the lower river's habitat and food web. "It's hard to believe what it was like down in the canyon," he said. "There were crayfish and lampreys and sculpins like you couldn't imagine." He says smelt spawned in the lower mile of the river, and clouds of insects hovered over the water in the evenings. "You wouldn't believe the caddis," he said.

All that food may explain why the Elwha supported such a strong population of resident trout. Unfortunately, much of it is gone. Smelt haven't been seen for years, and the lamprey and crayfish and sculpins are also largely lost. You still see nice hatches of blue-winged olives, pale morning duns, yellow sallies and *Rhyacophila* caddis, and they can provide fine dry fly-fishing. After the dams are removed, however, the ability of the middle and upper river's rainbows to compete with juvenile anadromous fish will probably depend largely on the river's largest insects—its salmonflies, golden stones and October caddis. Their nymphs and larvae provide adult rainbow and juvenile steelhead a sizable, nutritious, year-round food source.

The late James Garrett's most well-known fly, his Black and Orange Olympic Stonefly, was created to imitate the Elwha's salmonfly nymphs. Garrett worked for the Washington Department of Fisheries in the 1970s and '80s, and lived at the Dungeness and Sol Duc hatcheries and worked occasionally on the Elwha. An exceptionally gifted fly-tier, Garrett created a number of dressings for Olympic Peninsula steelhead and salmon, and taught fly-tying at Peninsula College and later at Manuel Bernardo's Quality Fly Fishing. Garrett's stonefly is an uncannily realistic imitation of the *Pteronarcys princeps* nymphs that are abundant on the Elwha. It is a fine pattern for rainbows on the middle and upper river, but J.D. Love, a good friend of Garrett's, says Garrett fished it primarily for summer steelhead on the lower river.

Searching for the right fly at the Elwha during late summer.

It was still legal to fish with bait on the Elwha when I first moved to the peninsula, and local bait-fishermen paid more attention to the river's large caddis than its stoneflies. I was always puzzled when I heard them talking about fishing "periwinkles." To me, a periwinkle was a cone-shaped mollusk, the ones you often see in shell collections. I eventually figured out that, at least on the peninsula, a periwinkle is also the name for the larval form of an October caddis. *Dicosmoecus* are widespread on the river, and they are one of the few insects large enough to impale on a hook and fish as bait. The fact that they were so popular with anglers is all the proof you need of their importance in the diet of Elwha trout.

"I was fishing in a canoe on Lake Mills years ago and it got too rough to paddle back and I had to camp overnight," said Ed Samuelson, whose family has lived on the peninsula for generations. "I caught a trout to eat, and it was stuffed with caddis larvae."

James Garrett never got to fish for summer steelhead above the dams, but many of his elegant summer steelhead dressings will be perfect for the middle and upper Elwha once summer fish return. Like Glasso before him, Garrett never fell under the thrall of hair-winged dressings for steelhead. He preferred teal and mallard and golden pheasant for wings, and floss and tinsel bodies. His low-water summer steelhead dressings like the Teresa's Tease seem more Canadian than American, and more 19th century than early 21st century. Garrett also created steelhead-sized soft hackles such as his Libby's Black, and his Septober Caddis Series imitated the October caddis in its various life stages.

You don't need to hike up to Elinor Chittenden's haunts to see the Elwha's summer steelhead potential. Just drive along the Olympic Hot Springs Road, the road that provides access to the middle river. You will pass deep green pools, shallow riffles and pocket water, boulder-strewn cascades, and alder-covered islands. You will see a lot of nice steelhead holding water from the road, but keep going until you cross the iron bridge a mile or so beyond the Elwha Ranger Station. Turn into Altaire Campground and drive to the walk-in campsites at the north end of the campground. Follow the fisherman's trail into the woods. You will climb a little knoll, then drop down to as sweet a piece of summer steelhead water as you are ever going to see.

The Elwha breaks out of an upstream rapids here, and flows broadly and shallowly over cobble, the deep channel hugging the alders on the far bank. Just downstream, it gathers and drops into a soft little gut. It then tails into a broad run, with seams and creases and gentle boils, that extends several hundred yards downstream, to the next patch of broken water. During summer, the gut and tailout are deep enough and slow enough to provide perfect holding water for steelhead resting between the rapids. It holds some nice rainbows now, but few people fish it, even though it's virtually within a campground. It's been waiting for the steelhead for 80 years.

Lots of October caddis hover above the water here in the fall, and it would be a great place to take a summer steelhead on Garrett's Septober Caddis. Then when someone asked you if you caught anything you could say, "Yeah, a steelhead."

"What on?" would be the inevitable second question.

"A periwinkle," you would say.

Garrett's Summer Steelhead Flies

Tied by Curtis Reed

Teresa's Tease

Tail: Golden pheasant crest, dyed hot-orange
Body: Red yarn
Front: Peacock palmered with soft hackle
Rib: Embossed gold tinsel, rear half
Throat: Guinea
Wing: Green-winged teal flank, drake

Septober Caddis-Male

Abdomen: Chenille, fluorescent orange, fine
Thorax: Otter
Hackle Hungarian partridge
Wing: Ring-neck pheasant philo plumes, dampened and pinched to length

Libby's Black

Body: Rear half, black floss; front half, black ostrich
Rib: Back half only, embossed silver
Hackle: Webby ring-neck pheasant belly, dyed black
Head: Purple head

Chapter Eight

Lake Crescent Trout

Lake Crescent is home to the unique Beardslee and crescenti trout.

This is what renowned trout authority Robert Behnke had to say about Lake Crescent in the Spring 1984 issue of Trout magazine: "If I were asked what Pacific Coast lake holds the largest nonanadromous rainbow and cutthroat trout, I would say Crescent Lake, Washington." Lake Crescent's "Beardslee" rainbows have been recorded to 20 pounds (16-pound official record) and its "crescenti" cutthroat have reached 12 pounds. They evolved from steelhead and sea-run cutthroat trapped in the 9-mile-long, 4300-acre lake after a massive landslide blocked its original outlet. Fjord-like Lake Crescent's dearth of spawning and nursery habitat produces small numbers of trout each year, but once they attain a foot or so in length, they wax fat on the lake's large population of kokanee salmon.

By the early 20th century, 11 fishing resorts on Lake Crescent catered to anglers from around the world. Although the lake was still highly productive, the state built a hatchery on Barnes Creek in 1913. Despite the release of 14 million hatchery fish over the next 62 years, genetic testing in the 1980s suggested that fish similar to the original Beardslee and crescenti trout still roamed the lake's depths. Since then, Olympic National Park has managed Lake Crescent trout with increasingly conservative regulations. It limited fishing to artificial lures in 1988 and implemented a 20-inch minimum size in 1994 to ensure fish spawned at least once before harvest. In 2000, surveys revealed low spawner numbers and new genetic information showed Beardslees were unlike any other coastal rainbow. The park responded with catch-and-release regulations, prohibited weights over two ounces, and delayed the opening date to June 1 to protect late spawners in Barnes Creek.

According to Sam Brenkman, Olympic National Park fisheries biologist, the spawner numbers of the lake's three wild stocks—Beardslee, crescenti cutthroat and a downriver cutthroat—responded quickly to the more restrictive management. "It really promotes the case for catch-and-release fishing in waters not subject to commercial harvest and where habitat is of high quality," he said. "In recent years, we have seen five or six times more Beardslee trout redds when compared to those counts from 1989 to 1992 when harvest was allowed." Brenkman also observed that Lake Crescent is different any other Olympic Peninsula lake. "It speaks to the uniqueness of Lake Crescent and its endemic trout populations as introduced species like lake trout and eastern brook didn't take there despite intensive hatchery planting. Brook trout have successfully adapted to many mountain lakes and rivers in the park but not Lake Crescent."

Last fall, I saw a solitary angler in a small rowboat on Lake Crescent. It was a misty morning, just after daybreak, and spectral fog hung over the water. I was heading west on Highway 101 for sea-runs on the lower Sol Duc and Bogachiel. As usual, I didn't see any boats between East Beach and Barnes Cove, but after I passed the grove of old-growth Douglas fir near Barnes Creek, I noticed the white boat. It was about 100 feet from shore. I could see a fly-rod in the stern, and an angler in rain gear and a sou'easter was working the oars.

"That guy knows what he's doing," I said to myself.

A few days later, I drove out to Forks again, this time to talk to Dick Wentworth. We talked about a lot of things that afternoon, not just Spey flies and steelhead, and at one point I mentioned Lake Crescent.

"I was out there the other day," Dick said.

"Were you in the white rowboat with the rain gear?"

Dick smiled. "That was me."

Dick caught fish to 18 inches that day, and he has caught much larger ones on flies. I'm not going to reveal any of his secrets. "People always want to get to the top of the mountain," he told me, "but they don't want to walk the trail." But he does have advice for anglers who want to improve their odds of taking big fish on Lake Crescent. "You've got to fish it like you do chinook," he said, with smile.

That's not how most fly-anglers approach Lake Crescent. They fish like they're after for trout, not big salmon, and as though they're on any other Olympic Peninsula lake. They fish near creek mouths. They cast small baitfish and attractor patterns. They are also pretty relaxed about when they get on the water. This is fine if you want to catch fish to 14 inches or so, which feed on insects and often cruise the shoreline. I occasionally fish Lake Crescent this way myself. It's a beautiful lake, and you can even buy a glass of wine at the Lake Crescent Lodge when you're done fishing. But it's not the way you fish for chinook in the Strait of Juan de Fuca, and it's not the way to connect with a big Lake Crescent trout.

Large chinook often feed near or on the surface just before and shortly after first light, and so do big Lake Crescent fish. This gives fly-fishers a shot at the big guys with a floating line or intermediate. Lake Crescent trout are also closer to the surface during spring and late fall, when the water is cooler. Anyone who has spent much time driving around the lake on the way to fish West End rivers during winter has seen large swirls in the murky pre-dawn light. One of the lake's regulars in the late 1800s, Theo Mallison from London, England, always arrived in March and stayed till May. You can't fish in spring or winter now, but you can fish all the way to Halloween.

As for flies, Olympic National Park released a report in 2002 that establishes something that the best Lake Crescent anglers have always known: Lake Crescent rainbows and cutthroat feed almost entirely on kokanee after they are around 14 inches long. Interestingly, these findings are similar to research in 1935 that found that large rainbow and cutthroat stomachs consisted "almost entirely of landlocked sockeye fingerlings, with very rarely a small trout." According to the new research, fish over 20 inches fed exclusively on kokanee. Although earlier studies found sculpins, whitefish and crayfish in the stomachs, the most recent study found none. In other words, if you want a big Lake Crescent trout, fish a big fly that looks like a juvenile kokanee.

And don't sleep in.

Chapter Nine

Dungeness Silver

When my wife, Eliana, and I were caretakers at the Dungeness National Wildlife Refuge, our cabin was just a couple miles from the mouth of the Dungeness River. During autumn, when coho were in the river, I would often drive over to the Dungeness early, before first light, and see how many cars were parked by the Schoolhouse Bridge. If there were more than one or two, I'd go home. The differences between what fly-fishers and gear- and bait-anglers consider "enough room" are wildly at odds, and I would rather not fish than be silently irritated or engage in a shouting match. Usually, there were at least half a dozen cars in the parking lot. You could depend on a crowd if a recent storm had brought the river up and pulled in fresh fish.

Headwaters of the Dungeness River.

I could hardly believe it, then, when the parking lot was empty one early November morning. A steady rain had fallen through the night, and there was a big pre-dawn high tide. I had been drowsily aware of the rain on the cabin's mossy shingles during the night, and each time I briefly woke, I though about the coho. I had been waiting for just this situation, but even though it was a weekday, I wasn't optimistic. As a corporate and military retirement haven, Sequim has a lot of people who don't have very much to do anymore.

The rain was still falling as I wriggled into my waders and strung my 8-weight. A stiff southern breeze ruffled the tops of the fir trees, and I could hear the reedy song of Canada geese, moving inland from Dungeness Bay to feed in the fields. It was just light enough to wade when I eased into the water. The river was up, pushing hard on my calves and ferrying alder branches and big-leaf maple leaves downstream. It was still in good shape, though, high but with good clarity. The rain and tide had brought in fish. I startled a pair of coho midstream, and they cut wild vees as they raced upstream.

In my experience, coho are most receptive to flies during the half hour before daybreak and immediately preceding darkness in the evening. I took up position upstream and to the side of a large snag on the east side of the river, near the end of the dike path. The current downcuts strongly around the snag, and coho like to hang in the softer deeper water behind it. I stripped about ten coils of line, and cast tight to the outside edge of the snag. The heavy sink-tip carried my orange and yellow marabou pattern, Jim Garrett's Dungeness Silver, down quickly. I let it drift into the deeper water until it began to hang, then retrieved it with sharp, fairly fast six-inch strips.

On about my sixth cast, I felt a strong tug, then a head shake. I reared back instinctively, probably too hard, and a salmon raced downstream. It peeled out of the shallows and into the main current. I let it go, just held the rod and let the weight of the line and rod work on it. It didn't jump. Suddenly, it wheeled and raced back upstream. Now, I was madly stripping line, trying to keep slack out. Fortunately, the fish angled away from me, to a deep pocket on the opposite side of the river. It scattered a solitary coho. By then I had the line back on the reel and regained tension on the fish. I landed it a few minutes later. It was a chunky buck, with just the trace of an enlarged nose, about eight pounds.

The headwaters of the Dungeness River and its major tributary, the Graywolf River, drop through one of the state's steepest watercourses. Once it leaves the mountains at Dungeness Forks Campground, the Dungeness also flows through the driest valley in the Pacific Northwest. Despite these challenging features, the Dungeness historically supported as many as 26,000 chinook and 450,000 pink salmon. It also hosted good runs of winter and summer steelhead, coho, three races of chum, and cutthroat and bull trout. Unfortunately, Dungeness chinook, bull trout and chum are now all listed as "'threatened" under the Endangered Species Act, and all of its stocks were described as "critical" in a 1995 status review by the Elwha Klallam Tribe.

The weak runs have resulted in extremely limited fishing opportunity in recent years. Indeed, the lower river currently closes at the end of the winter steelhead season on February 28 and does not open again until mid-October. You aren't really missing much. It never had a resident rainbow fishery comparable to the Elwha's. Its cutthroat have been essentially nonexistent for decades, and the state no longer plants summer steelhead. Around 200 hatchery winter steelhead are taken annually, but coho provide by far the bulk of the sport harvest. Almost all of them are hatchery fish, bound for the WDFW Dungeness Salmon Hatchery at RM 11. During a good year, anglers take as many as 4,000 5- to 15-pound fish.

For a fly-fisher, it takes a little ingenuity to have an enjoyable time on the Dungeness these days. Word gets around fast when a fresh pulse of silvers are in, and pretty soon well-known public access points are full of old trucks with Confederate flag decals and Cadillac SUVs. But there is a lot of public access between the mouth and the salmon deadline at the hatchery. Your best bet is to check all of it every morning when conditions are good. Also, don't be afraid to walk, because most of your competitors won't. The main thing is to grab an opening when you see it. Believe me, on the Dungeness someone will show up soon.

Rivers

Salt Creek: Historically a fine winter steelhead and coho stream, Salt Creek is pretty much a sea-run creek today. It flows into salt marsh at Crescent Bay. Intertidal access at Salt Creek Recreation Area, DNR holdings upstream, and along spurs off Camp Hayden Road.

Lyre River: Lake Crescent's outflow, the Lyre River is only five miles long and a falls at RM 3 blocks anadromous fish from the upper river. Nonetheless, it hosted a strong chum run, winter steelhead, sea-run cutthroat, and a small summer steelhead stock. In recent years, winter steelhead have provided the only dependable fishing. Lake Crescent's unique Beardslee rainbow spawn in the outlet, and ONP and the WDFW have implemented catch-and-release and selective fishery regulations above the falls. Access is available at the DNR's Lyre River Campground, at the Lyre River Resort (access fee) and timber company and DNR land above the 112 bridge. There is little good fly-water.

Elwha River: Draining more than 321 square miles, the Elwha is the peninsula's fourth-largest river, and the Strait of Juan de Fuca's largest tributary. It rises on the southeast side of the Mount Olympus and the Bailey Range, and is partly glacial, although less so than the Queets or Hoh. That means that it blows out after heavy winter storms and can be cloudy on the June opener when the nearby Sol Duc is clear. Before two dams without fish-passage facilities were built on the lower and middle river in the early 20th century, the Elwha hosted all 10 species of North Pacific salmon and trout. Summer chinook grew to 100 pounds, steelhead swam deep into the backcountry, and pink, coho, sockeye and chum swarmed into the lower river. The dams are scheduled to begin coming down by 2012. That will open the 83 percent of the ecosystem above the lower dam to migratory fish, most of it in Olympic National Park wilderness. Until then, anglers can divide the river into three sections. The lower river, the 4.9 miles below the Elwha Dam, is available to anadromous fish, but hatchery coho and winter steelhead have been the only things open in recent years. The lower river has been closed to all fishing during summer recently to protect ESA-listed chinook. Access is available from the WDFW Elwha Rearing Channe (Map A23), at the Sisson Access (Map A22), and off Place Road at the mouth. The middle reach, which extends from the upper end of Lake Aldwell to the Glines Canyon Dam, is rainbow trout water. The average is about 10 inches, but fish to 16 inches are taken. The middle river is paralleled closely by the Elwha Hot Springs Road, and turn-outs provide easy access to the state and park water. The water above Lake Mills is only accessible by trail, and most of it is covered in the Backcountry section. However, fit day-hikers can reach several miles of fine trout water by hiking into Geyser Valley. The Elwha River Trail hangs high above the river, but spur trails take you down to the valley. When the dams finally come down, the river will be closed for five years to give salmon and migratory trout time to reestablish themselves in the middle and upper river.

Morse Creek: Located on the eastern edge of Port Angeles, Morse Creek tumbles off the steep northern face of the Olympics. From a passing car, it's an unprepossessing stream, but historically it supported large runs of winter steelhead, cutthroat, and several species of salmon. It even had spring chinook, the smallest Olympic Peninsula river with a springer run. As recently as the 1980s, Morse Creek was still a fine winter-steelhead stream, but harvest figures have declined dramatically. A few fish are taken, but few people pursue them.

Dungeness River: The only major Olympic Peninsula river whose name is not of Indian origin, the Dungeness was named by George Vancouver for the Dungeness Point region of southern England. Once one of the region's richest and most diverse migratory fish systems, the Dungeness supported strong runs of chinook and coho, two stocks of pink salmon, native char, summer and winter steelhead, and probably three stocks of chum. Today, it's one of the peninsula's most degraded rivers, and fishing opportunity is limited. The entire river below Dungeness Forks Campground is closed through summer and early autumn to protect chinook salmon. It does produce the Strait of Juan de Fuca's largest run of hatchery coho, and the mid-October opener draws big crowds. Hatchery winter steelhead provide a modest fishery, but finding room for fly-fishing is difficult on easily accessible portions of the river. The traditional June 1 opener remains in effect above Dungeness Forks, and small rainbow are available above Dungeness Forks and from the Upper Dungeness trail (Map A18). On the lower river, access is available at the Dungeness Salmon Hatchery (RM 10.8), at Clallam County's Three Waters County Park (Map A16) (off Taylor Cutoff Road) and Wheeler River Park (Map A14) (off Ward Road), at the Railroad Bridge Park (Map A15) off Priest Road, and above and below the old Dungeness School (Map A13) near the mouth.

Graywolf River: On its free-fall from the high country to Dungeness Forks, the Graywolf drops nearly 6,000 feet—the steepest watercourse of any major Washington river. The Lower Graywolf Trail (Map A17) provides access to the river at several locations but is also frequently above or away from the river. It's worth remembering during hot spells, because the Graywolf is at a higher elevation than other easily accessible rivers, and flows nearly entirely beneath a canopy of cooling fir and cedar. Currently, the bridge 4.2 miles from the trailhead is out. You may see pinks or catch a char on the Graywolf, but trout are the only thing you can legally pursue. As on the neighboring Elwha, resident rainbow provide the sport, and cutthroat are virtually nonexistent. Ten inches is about average, and anything over 12 is a nice fish. But Waters West's Curt Reed took a 20-incher a few years ago, and you just know there are other big fish beneath the log jams and in inaccessible canyon pools.

Snow and Salmon Creeks: These rivers flow into the head of Discovery Bay. They look appealing as cutthroat, coho and chum streams, but have been off limits since the 1970s. The WDFW conducts long-term research and monitoring projects on both rivers at its Snow Creek Research Facility.

Chimacum Creek: Chimacum Creek (Map A6) is the Quimper Peninsula's only significant fish system, but nearly all of it is privately owned and there is little river fishing. However, it is the mother stream for the sea-runs that provide much of the saltwater cutthroat fishing in Port Townsend Bay and around Indian Island. There is some fishing at the mouth but the creek is too deep and soft to wade, and the bank upstream is slippery and bordered by bluffs. But anglers with canoes or kayaks can launch at the WDFW property off Moore Street in Irondale (the old road that led into the creek is gated), paddle north to the estuary, and into the creek on a rising tide. Just don't forget to get out well before the tide turns, because the creek is a trickle on summer low tides. The lower river closes at the end of August to protect its summer chum.

Ludlow Creek: Although only 4.5 miles long, Ludlow Creek drains a 17-square-mile basin that includes Ludlow and Horseshoe lakes and a number of ponds. A waterfall a half mile above the mouth blocks anadromous fish at most flows, but native cutthroat inhabit the upper river. The basin contains beaver ponds, but it takes a lot of work to find them and many have blown out or dried up during the recent drought years.

Rain Shadow Lakes

Lake Crescent (Lake Crescent): Filling a glacier-carved basin at the base of Mount Storm King and Pyramid Peak, fjord-like Lake Crescent is nearly nine miles long and has more than 5,100 surface acres. It is also deep and oligotrophic—that is, infertile and with scant shallow-water habitat for juvenile trout. The lake's native Beardslee rainbow and crescenti cutthroat have nonetheless adapted elegantly to these constraints, and 20-pound Beardslees (16-pound official record) and 12-pound cutts have been documented. Kokanee are the forage base for the large fish. Responding to concerns about declining spawner numbers and recent genetic research that indicated Beardslee rainbow are unlike any other rainbows, ONP has banned weights over 2 ounces (effectively eliminating downriggers), delayed the season until June 1, and implemented catch-and-release regulations. Since then, the numbers of fish seen during snorkel surveys have increased dramatically. Fly-fishers usually concentrate on creek mouths and points, and fish streamers and leech patterns. Park Service boat launches are located at Barnes Point and Fairholm.

Lake Sutherland (Elwha): Originally part of Lake Crescent before it was separated from the larger lake by an enormous landslide thousands of years ago, 360-acre Lake Sutherland drains east via Indian Creek to the Elwha. Sockeye swam up the creek to the lake before the lower Elwha Dam was built. Today, hatchery rainbow and wild cutthroat are its attractions, and the State releases about 10,000 legal rainbows in early and mid-spring, along with a few hundred larger fish. Although 12-inchers are standard, 2-pound holdover rainbows are caught. Even larger cutthroat, some to 7 pounds, have been taken. Surrounded by cottages and summer homes, the lake is a playground for water skiers and jet skis during summer, but some of the best fishing occurs in early spring (it is open year-round) and after Labor Day. There is limited bank fishing, but a boat launch is located off the South Shore Road.

Anderson Lake (Chimacum): Located within Anderson Lake State Park, a couple miles west of Port Hadlock, Anderson Lake has been an early season Jefferson County favorite for decades. Surrounded by forest, rocky outcrops, and marsh, the 58-acre lake is fertile enough the state doesn't usually plant it with catchable fish until after the opener. It typically gets around 30,000 rainbow fry, which grow into 12-inchers by the following spring, along with around 5,000 adult rainbow in May. It is open to harvest and all types of angling from the late April opener through August, but is catch-and-release and under selective fishery regulations in September and October. Holdovers to 18 inches are taken. Some larger trout have red flesh, suggesting the presence of scuds. The park has a fee boat launch.

Gibbs Lake (Chimacum): You didn't see that many fly-fishers on this 36-acre lowland lake until it switched over to catch-and-release for trout and began to receive several hundred triploid rainbows each spring. Now it is a darling of fly clubs. Unfortunately, the lake also contains bass, which can be retained. Fortunately, they tend to hang out around the lily pads and snags near shore, while the trout prefer the open water. Sea-run cutthroat and coho occasionally make it to the lake when its outlet, Naylor's Creek, has enough flow. That suggests fry and smolt patterns may be worth a try. There is no ramp but you can launch float tubes and car-toppers from the county park.

Ludlow Lake (Ludlow): Ludlow Lake (15 acres) is located on Pope Resources property a few miles west of the Hood Canal Bridge. All types of gear are legal, and hatchery rainbows provide most of the action. It receives approximately 1,000 legal rainbows in March, and anglers fish it hard in spring. The forest road into Ludlow Lake, which forks off Sandy Shore Lake Road, just north of SR 104, is usually open.

Horseshoe Lake (Ludlow): Although it is only a couple of miles down the road from Ludlow Lake, Horseshoe Lake is usually less crowded and more likely to attract fly-fishers. That's because it is a selective fishery lake, with a one-fish daily bag. It also receives around 150 triploids each April. Access is the same as for Ludlow Lake, but the road can be gated during logging operations.

Teal Lake: Located off Teal Lake Road between Highway 104 and Port Ludlow, 15-acre Teal Lake has been more or less adopted by the retired corporate high-fliers in Port Ludlow. The State plants around 1,500 legal rainbows in March and April, along with 100 larger fish. Fish over five pounds have been taken. It has a fishing dock and ramp. The lake is open in winter but the regulations are complicated, so check the pamphlet.

Section 3

Oyster Country

Fly originated and tied by Doug Rose.

Widgeon Girl

Hook: Tiemco 3761; size 8-12
Body: Pearsall's marabou floss, green
Hackle Support: Brown dubbing
Wing: Widgeon flank feathers, male
Head: Red thread

MAP B: Oyster Country

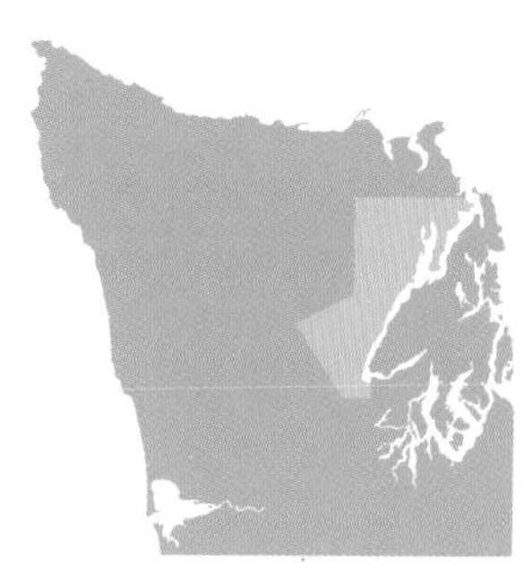

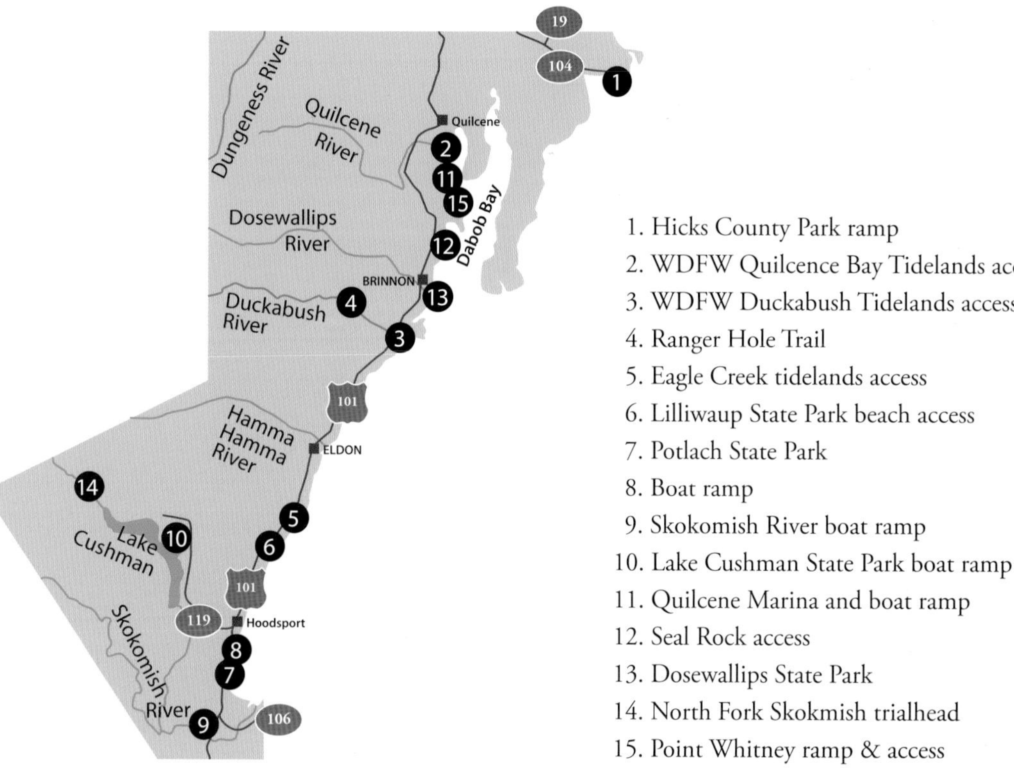

1. Hicks County Park ramp
2. WDFW Quilcence Bay Tidelands access
3. WDFW Duckabush Tidelands access
4. Ranger Hole Trail
5. Eagle Creek tidelands access
6. Lilliwaup State Park beach access
7. Potlach State Park
8. Boat ramp
9. Skokomish River boat ramp
10. Lake Cushman State Park boat ramp
11. Quilcene Marina and boat ramp
12. Seal Rock access
13. Dosewallips State Park
14. North Fork Skokmish trialhead
15. Point Whitney ramp & access

Chapter Ten

The Lake at the Head of the Swamp

Gibbs Lake is another popular East Side trout lake.

You don't have to be a fly-fisher to fall in love with Price Lake. Nestled beneath the timbered foothills of the southeast Olympics, bordered on the south by Dow Mountain and north by Saddle Mountain, it is as beautiful a low-elevation lake as you will ever see. I have been there on days when it was so still, so utterly, breathlessly calm, that it was hard to tell the difference between the trees above the lake and the reflection of the trees on the water. There is no development, and you can't even see it from the road. In a very real sense, it gives anglers a glimpse of what many low-elevation Olympic Peninsula lakes looked like before settlement. It is also a selective fishery lake, with catch-and-release regulations, which makes it a favorite of fly-fishers.

Although Price Lake has more than enough charms to impress non-anglers, I don't imagine very many ever see it. It's in the South Fork of the Lilliwaup Creek basin, between

Potlatch and Lake Cushman. It isn't on the road to anywhere, and since the spur road off FR 25 near Melbourne Lake that previously provided access is now blocked, anglers from the north have to drive all the way to Hoodsport and SR 119 to reach the lake. The DNR's 1000 Road forks off SR 119 near Lake Cushman State Park, and the 1100 Road takes you about two miles to the lake. Almost no one but anglers and hunters drive this road, and it is gated during winter and early spring to protect the Lilliwaup Valley's elk herd.

Actually, Price's utterly undeveloped appearance is deceptive, because it has a long and storied fly-fishing history. The Price Lake Resort operated on the southwest corner of the lake between 1920 and around 1970. It let cabins and rented rowboats and sold tackle. Enos Bradner fished the lake regularly, and he and his partner, Frank Headrick, created the Dandy Green Nymph for Price Lake fish in springtime.

"I grew up fishing Price Lake," said Rick Endicott, who is now a hatchery manager with Long Live the Kings. "My grandfather opened the resort in the 1920s. Before that he was a fire lookout for a logging company on Dow Mountain. He lived in a cabin on the lake from the 1920s into the 50s, and my mother was born at the lake. I actually lived there in a cabin for a while after I got out of high school. There were still a couple of rowboats when I was a kid. I fished it a lot until 1980."

According to Rick, the resort was on the upper end of the lake, the west shore. "You came into it on a really beautiful board walk," he said. "It had cedar posts and hand-cut end planks. It was about a quarter mile long through the swamp. When I was young, several rowboats were still for rent but a lot were sunk in the shallows. There were several cabins. We used to tie our own flies. We mostly fished Royal Coachman and Mosquitos. We would row around the lake and cast up to shore. The east side was better for fly-fishing."

Not unexpectedly, habitat is the reason the lake was so productive in the days of the resort, and despite recent downturns it still turns out fish to four pounds. The logs and snags along the shore provide cover for juvenile fish. They also serve as emerging platforms for damselflies and dragonflies and as carpenter ant lodging. The lake has floating vegetation on the east and west ends, and it is one of the few Olympic lakes with extensive mats of submerged weeds. These produce strong populations of subaquatic insects and scuds, some reaching nearly one inch. Cutthroat and brook trout spawn naturally in the lake, mostly in the gravel at the outlet.

Most of the effort directed at Price Lake today occurs in spring, between the late April opener and early June, and again in fall, when its trout feed eagerly in anticipation of winter. It can provide fine fishing during early summer, though, and you are much less likely to have competition. I was the only person on the lake the last time I fished it, a weekday before most schools were out.

The *Callibaetis* mayflies that had kept fly-fishers busy a few weeks earlier were still around, but so were the damselflies and dragonflies that had brought me to the lake. Both damsels and dragons are meatier and emerge more predictably than the smaller early season insects, and the sight of them moving through the shallows often draws the attention of substantial trout. Because they hatch later in the spring and continue to emerge through summer, they are a good bet in June.

I fished a damselfly nymph that morning, at the end of an intermediate line and 12-foot leader. Dragonfly nymphs are larger, and I could have begun with a big juicy fat-butted dragonfly pattern. But I have always had more strikes on the slender, olive, three-tailed damselfly nymphs. I also like the way you fish them—stripping slowly, but steadily just beneath the surface, imitating their migrations from the bottom to the emergent vegetation and snags where they emerge. It is more fun than the deep, erratic, stop and go that is productive with dragonfly nymphs.

I caught a fish quickly that day along the snaggy shoreline west of the launch. It wasn't a tremendous trout—about 11 inches—but it jumped and fought hard right to the float tube. When I saw that it was a cutthroat, I was happy. Rainbow and cutthroat and eastern brooks have all been stocked in the lake, and they have persisted, even thrived in its rich, soupy waters. But cutthroat are the fish that belong in Price Lake.

"I've got a report from June of 1932 on the lake," Endicott said. "It says the creek (Lilliwaup) was 'well stocked' with eastern brook, and that cutthroat were 'exceptionally well-stocked' in the stream and lake."

Dragonfly nymphs are also productive in autumn, and some anglers take fish on floating dragonfly dressings. Trout in most lakes don't seem to show much interest in adult dragonflies, but Price Lake trout occasionally hit them hard. However, they prefer the red-bodied insects, which have shorter and stumpier bodies, not the more common blue or green ones. The presentation is straightforward: Cast toward shore, let it sit, twitch it, let it sit again, and then work it back toward the float tube. If you do this often enough, you may eventually experience a real jolt.

Finally, the trail from the road down to the lake isn't very long but it is steep, and you don't want to carry anything too heavy. That definitely precludes boats, unless you are young and tough and have a friend. Price Lake is really the realm of float tubes or small rafts today, and rafts are safer because they keep you above the myriad snags, some of them sharp, along the shore. Blowdown also occasionally covers the trail, and it can be a chore to drag even a float tube around the trail and through the brush. The put-ins at the lake aren't that great either, and they are often muddy and deeper than you think. Be careful.

Chapter Eleven

North Fork Skokomish

Kevin Ryan fishing tidewater on the Skokomish.

The fishing regulations for the North Fork of the Skokomish River in Olympic National Park can seem a little strange if you don't know the rationale behind them. The season opens on June 1, as do most of the major rivers on the Peninsula, but it closes on September 15. This is a full six weeks earlier than rivers like the Elwha or the forks of the Quinault or the upper portions of the neighboring Dosewallips or Duckabush rivers. It's easy to forget this, and each fall I decide to drive down to Staircase and spend a few hours rock-hopping with a Royal Wulff. Then I remember the river is closed. This year I did remember, but access to the North Fork Skokomish Trailhead was closed as a result of the Bear Gulch Fire.

The early closing date is to protect the river's bull trout. When Lt. Joseph O'Neil led the first trail building and scientific exploration of the North Fork Skokomish upstream of Lake Cushman in 1890, the river supported Hood Canal's strongest runs of salmon, as well as winter and summer steelhead, and sea-run cutthroat. It was also noted for its native char. "I was always very successful, especially toward evening, for fish are abundant in the lake, both brook-trout and bull trout," Louis F. Henderson, the O'Neil Expedition botanist, wrote in his journal. "The latter take the spoon greedily, even after a hearty meal. I caught one about two feet long, and on preparing it for the cook I found in its stomach a whole trout eight inches long."

All of the North Fork's migratory fish began a long, slow downward spiral when a hydroelectric dam without fish-passage facilities was built downstream of Lake Cushman in the 1920s. But the descendants of Henderson's "bull trout" still swim in the lake, which was greatly expanded from its original size by the upper dam, and in the North Fork above the lake. Many of these fish have an adfluvial life history, which means that they spawn and rear in the river but spend considerable time feeding in Lake Cushman.

The lower Skokomish River.

Skokomish River bull trout are the last surviving bull trout stock native to the Hood Canal basin, but they have definitely experienced difficulties in recent years. According to Park Service snorkel surveys, approximately 400 adult bull trout were counted in the stream in 1973, but those numbers fell to 125 two years later and to 70 in 1977. The park responded with catch-and-release regulations for bull trout in 1985. Fewer than 50 fish were recorded in 1987, and hardly any were seen in 1989. But the numbers began a dramatic turn-around in 1991, when 300 fish were observed, and 400 were reported two years later. However, snorkel and tagging studies showed that bull trout from Lake Cushman begin to migrate upstream in early October. That's why the park shortened the season to mid September.

There are plenty of other places to fish on the Olympic Peninsula in fall, and the best time to cast a fly on the North Fork is probably early to midsummer anyway. While the river does have some glacial input, it cleans up faster during the spring than the Elwha, the other park river with resident trout above dams without fish-passage facilities. It is usually fishable by mid-June. The North Fork Skokomish Trail is also low elevation and is nearly always accessible in early summer. The trailhead at the Staircase Ranger Station and Campground is at 785 feet, and it only climbs to 1,475 feet in the 3.8 miles to the Flapjack Lakes Trail. You can craft a nice day hike and fishing trip on the North Fork without expending either a lot of sweat or time.

Rainbow and cutthroat are both available. The average is probably eight inches and anything over a foot is a nice one. They hold behind rocks and sweepers, at the base of plunge pools, along the foam lines against cliffs and clay banks, and in the soft water on the deep side of gravel bars. You won't need anything but a floating line. You may see pale morning duns, small caddis and yellow sallies and golden stones, but I wouldn't worry too much about imitating them. A small fly box with a selection of Parachute Adams, Elk Hair Caddis, Royal Wulffs, Prince Nymphs, Gold Ribbed Hare's Ears, Muddler Minnows, small Woolly Buggers and soft hackles are all you need.

The North Fork of the Skokomish is a place to have fun, not to worry about matching bugs or perfectly presenting a Lady Caroline on the greased line. Pack a nice lunch. Stop at Hama Hama Seafood and buy some smoked salmon and crab, and a bottle of beer in Hoodsport. Wear hip boots rather than waders. Fish upstream with dry flies, then turn around and fish back down with wet flies. Take your time. Enjoy the Douglas squirrels, ratcheting their displeasure at your presence. Watch the band-tailed pigeons feeding on the red elderberry. When log jams or rapids make wading impossible, get out of the water and hike until you find another promising stretch.

Chapter Twelve

Saltmarsh Cutthroat

Fishing a soft hackle on a saltmarsh cutthroat creek.

A few years ago, Ron Hirschi regularly seined Hood Canal estuaries as part of a research project on the migratory pathways and timing of juvenile salmon. He called me one September afternoon and said that he had seen some "really big" cutthroat in a tidal pool on our favorite cutthroat creek.

"You should go fish it tomorrow," he said.

"Can you come?"

"I've got to work," he said. "But you go. It's a perfect tide, a big pre-dawn high."

It is a sweet little creek, tannin-colored but clear, only about a cast wide but deceptively deep. The tide runs upstream a good half mile from the canal, and big tides temporarily reverse its flow. The bank is too wet and salty for trees, but snags from upstream forests create instream structure. Saltgrass, pickleweed and Pacific silverweed provide the ground cover, and merciless tangles of hard hack, tules and cattails snag errant back casts. Beavers have worked the creek for generations, leaving runs and relict dams and old flats.

You often see gray otter scat, filled with fish bones, along the bank, and mallards, teal and Canada geese nest in the tules.

It was drizzling lightly, with scudding, charcoal clouds, when I got to the creek at daybreak the next morning. I got into my waders quickly and then, holding my 5-weight behind me, crawled through a tunnel of Himalaya blackberries to the edge of the creek. The water was still high from the tide, but the flow had turned back downstream. I followed the duck hunters' path upstream, trying to avoid falling into old beaver runs and over snags. At one point I had to quick-step through about 40 feet of sticky mud. I used to be able to do this sort of thing more gracefully, but I'm older and fatter now and just sort of blunder through them like an old blind bear. I stopped at the big flat where the creek doglegs to the left. Cutthroat fresh from the salt love to hold in it.

An early October tidewater cutthroat.

I tied on a fly of my own, a Widgeon Girl. It's a simple soft hackle, sort of like a Grouse and Green except I use Pearsall's Marabou floss for the body and widgeon for the wing. The flank feathers of a drake widgeon are a mottled pinkish russet color, and I think they may suggest the small shrimp that cutthroat feed on in salt water. I used a regular weight-forward floating line on the creek for years, but have recently switched to a Cortland Camo intermediate. It doesn't land as softly as a floater and it's harder to untangle if you snag the hard hack, but I am convinced it is less visible to the fish. Because I usually need to horse trout away from vegetation and occasionally hook coho, I use a 3X tippet, and I don't worry much as it gets thicker during the day.

I shanked my first cast that morning, a truly woebegotten tangle. Fortunately, even sea-runs fresh from salt water seem extraordinarily forgiving. I caught a 14-inch fish two casts later. It still had the sheen of the sea on him, without a trace of the cutthroat's eponymous throat slashes. A few casts later I connected with a heavier fish. It peeled line, and for a moment I thought I had a silver. But then it began to thrash and dive and make short jabbing runs. I brought it to the bank twice before I saw it clearly. It was a cutthroat, an honest 18-incher, with thick shoulders, purple splashes on its gill plates, and spots all the way to its belly.

"Thank you, Mr. Hirschi," I said out loud, after I released it.

I'm not going to tell you the name of that creek. That may be a novel premise in a fly-fishing guidebook, but the creek can't take a lot of pressure and, besides, the salmon-restoration folks have pretty much ruined it. But the Olympic Peninsula contains a host of creeks and rivers where you can fish for tidewater cutthroat—Salt Creek on the Strait of Juan de Fuca, the Little Hoquiam on Gray's Harbor, and the Quillayute River on the coast. The lower reaches of every major Hood Canal tributary flow through saltmarsh, and the Big Quilcene, Dosewallips, Duckabush, and Skokomish all have varying degrees of public access.

Fly-fishing for cutthroat in tidewater can be maddening, but it isn't complicated. You may take fish from midsummer on, but it is usually best in September and October. You can often extend the season on Rain Shadow and Hood Canal rivers that remain open after October, because cutthroat hang around spawning chum salmon looking for loose eggs. Some people like incoming water, when cutthroat ride the making tide into the creeks like surfers. Others prefer to concentrate on fish that have stacked up in tidal pools after the runout. I do it both ways, and they both work if the fish are around and are in the mood to bite. If I had to pick a favorite, it would be the situation I described at the beginning—a high tide a couple of hours before daylight.

Sea-runs fresh from salt water like cover. Pools, soft water behind snags and sweepers, and cuttbanks are always worth several casts. You don't see many cutthroat patterns with green, but I do very well with my Widgeon Girl.

A chartreuse-bodied Carey Special is also a good tidewater pattern, as are soft hackles with green floss or peacock herl bodies. The old standards such as the Knutson Spider (yellow or black body), Spruce fly, Purple Joe, Royal Coachman (bucktail and traditional feather-winged streamer) and Haig-Brown's Silver Lady and Silver Brown remain productive. You almost always fish downtide. Sometimes letting the fly swing and drift in the current works best, but I usually retrieve the fly.

You never know what you will encounter on tidewater creeks in autumn. Last fall, Ron Hirschi fished the creek at the beginning of the story and heard hissing and thrashing behind him. When he turned around he saw a black bear. It didn't seem very happy.

"It was a big one," he said. "Probably 200 pounds. It was shaking its head from side to side and sort of grunting."

"What did you do?" I asked.

"I left."

Rivers

Thorndyke Creek: Thorndyke Creek heads up in Sandy Shore Lake and flows through Pope Resources timberlands before draining in Thorndyke Bay. There is no easy access anywhere along its six-mile mainstem, and access to the estuary is prohibited (and guarded). But anglers willing to hike from gated log roads off the South Point Road (Thorndyke) or Coyle roads can get close to the creek. Small resident cutthroat and the occasional sea-run are available.

Tarboo Creek: As with most small Hood Canal tributaries, cutthroat are the only legal fly-fishing targets. There is little creek fishing, which may be just as well, because Tarboo Creek is the major tributary flowing into Tarboo Bay. As such, it provides many of the cutthroat taken by saltwater anglers in Dabob Bay.

Little Quilcene River: The Little Quil, as its known locally, drops quickly on its 12-mile course from Mount Townsend to the head of Quilcene Bay. Although it is called a river—and historically supported everything from chinook to steelhead and perhaps even pink salmon—the Little Quil is really a creek. Not that many people fish it and those that do must be content with palm-sized resident cutthroat and the rare sea-run.

Big Quilcene: The Big Quil flows into the west shore of Quilcene Bay less than two miles from the mouth of its sister river. It is a much larger system, however, with 19 miles of mainstem and major tributaries like Tunnel Creek, Townsend Creek and Penny Creek. The portion above the falls at RM 4 is primarily Forest Service land, and resident trout are the targets. The WDFW used to plant the canyon waters below the Quilcene Dam with hatchery rainbows but stopped in the 1990s. The overwhelming bulk of the effort on the Big Quil today is focused on the early fall run of hatchery coho to the Quilcene National Fish Hatchery. Fly-fishers should be advised that they comprise a nearly invisible minority here when coho are available, and anyone with delicate sensibilities should avoid the river entirely. Sea-run cutthroat are available in the lower river, but the section below Rogers Street is closed from midsummer through October to protect summer chum, which are listed under the ESA. Linger Longer Road in Quilcene provides access to the lower river, as do parking spaces by the Highway 101 bridge. The upper river can be reached by FR 27, a one-lane paved road, and its spurs.

Dosewallips River: The Twana Indian word for the Dosewallips means "river with two mouths," and the Dosey indeed splits below Highway 101. Although both McLeod (1940) and Bradner (1950) talk of its fine run of winter steelhead, chum salmon are its main draw today. The season opens November 1 and usually runs through December 15. They are only open from the Highway 101 bridge downstream to the mouth, and Dosewallips State Park provides access. The river re-opens June 1 and you can fish through August, but very few trout are available in the park reach or the section of river accessible from the Dosewallips River Road. The WDFW has even closed the winter steelhead season to protect the river's struggling wild stock. Dosewallips Falls is the upstream reach of anadromous fish, and a recent survey by ONP staff only found resident rainbow in the mainstem above the falls. The Dosewallips River Road has been blocked since 2003 by a washout five miles downstream of ONP's Dosewallips Campground. Hikers can negotiate a steep trail around the washout and return to the road, but the river is usually milky during the summer and its trout are small.

Duckabush River: The Duckabush historically hosted all the salmonids native to large west-side Hood Canal systems, including summer and winter steelhead, all salmon species save sockeye, and sea-runs. Today, its most productive fisheries focus on fall chum in the lower river and resident trout above the end of the road. The WDFW owns a large parcel just south of the Highway 101 bridge that provides access to the intertidal zone above the bridge, and the estuary and salt marsh at the mouth. Chum can be taken from both areas in November and early December, and they are relatively lightly fished. Pay attention to tide, because it can come in quickly, especially during big storms. Few trout are taken from the water accessible along the Duckabush River Road, and winter steelhead are now off limits. Hikers on the Duckabush River Trail can find some river access from informal way trails, but there are also box canyons. It isn't really worth your time until you get beyond the reach of a day hike.

Hamma Hamma: With an 18-mile mainstem and 85-square-mile basin, the Hamma Hamma is a major Hood Canal river, but a large falls blocks migratory fish access above RM 1.8. It nonetheless historically supported strong runs of salmon, which apparently gave the river its Indian name, "stinky stinky." The lower river and estuary are private property and permission to fish is not granted. Trout were hauled into the upper basin by the turn of the century, and the 1940 Ben Paris guide described the upper river as providing "exceptionally good fly-fishing for cutthroat and eastern brook from July on." Those days are long gone. The WDFW discontinued rainbow plants in the 1990s, and today a few resident brookies and cutthroat are taken in the more inaccessible reaches above Lena Creek. The 25 Road provides access to the north bank above Waketicheh Creek.

Fulton/Eagle/Jorsted: These three creeks flow into the canal between the Hamma Hamma and Skokomish. A generation ago, anglers took coho, chum and cutthroat in the lower ends, and resident and beaver pond trout higher up. Virtually all of the lower reaches are posted today, and few anglers bother to hike beyond gates into the timber company holdings upstream.

Lilliwaup Creek: One of Hood Canal's more intriguing watersheds, Lilliwaup Creek drains 17 square miles of wetlands, beaver ponds and swamps on its seven-mile journey from Price Lake to Hood Canal. An impassible falls at RM .7 prevents anadromous fish from penetrating the bulk of the basin, but resident cutthroat are available in the mainstem, the north and south forks, and beaver ponds. Other than at a couple of road crossings, however, the creek is tough to find, let alone fish, and not many people attempt it. In addition, many of the ponds and wetlands have dried up during the recent series of dry summers. The 24 Road flanks the upper end of the North Fork and the 1100 Road from Lake Cushman parallels the South Fork downstream of the Price Lake. However, the 1100 Road is blocked near Melbourne Lake on the north and a short distance beyond Price Lake.

Skokomish River: The largest river flowing into Hood Canal, the Skokomish was also Hood Canal's most productive anadromous fish system. Its North Fork rises in the high country of Olympic National Park and flows through a series of narrow canyons and Lake Cushman before merging with the South Fork near Potlach. Tacoma Power and Light's Cushman Dams have blocked migratory fish from 84 percent of the North Fork since 1926. The dams also essentially drain eight miles of the North Fork and divert approximately 96 percent of its annual flow. The South Fork heads up in the park below Sundown Pass, but it enters Olympic National Forest quickly. The mainstem is nine miles long and is bordered by the Skokomish Indian Reservation, farms and private residences. Although the Skokomish's fish runs are but a glimmer of what they were before the era of dams and clearcuts, it is the only Hood Canal tributary with an open season for chinook and coho salmon. A few winter steelhead are taken in the mainstem, and sea-run cutthroat drift in and out of the mouth during summer and fall. "I caught the biggest cutthroat of my life off the mouth of the Skokomish in the 1960s," said Joe Uhlman. The WDFW's Olympic Wildlife Area provides access to the mouth, and a boat launch is located upstream of the Highway 101 bridge. Resident trout are available in both forks. The lower end of the North Fork Skokomish Trail and Staircase Rapids Trail parallel the lower North Fork in the park. Forest Road 23 and its spurs provide access to the South Fork and the upper and low trailheads of the South Fork Skokomish Trail.

Lakes

Sandy Shore Lake (Thorndyke): Thirty-six-acre Sandy Shore Lake is located on Pope Resources land south of SR 104. It is deeper (60-foot maximum) than nearby lakes, and tends to hold up better during summer. Unfortunately, jet skis and power boats can make things miserable on sunny weekends. The State plants legal and triploid rainbows in spring, and contains some nice holdovers.

Silent Lake (Dabob Bay): This small, forested Toandos Peninsula lake is a lovely place to spend an autumn afternoon. It also gets a small plant of adult rainbows, and a few eastern brook trout roam the lake. The road to the boat ramp is fairly steep.

Tarboo Lake (Tarboo): Yet another lake on Pope timberlands, 21-acre Tarboo Lake is located west of Center Road, at the end of Tarboo Lake Road. Like Sandy Shore Lake, Tarboo can come on slowly in spring, but can provide decent fishing through summer. The State plants rainbows in spring, and the lake seems to contain more than the usual number of 14-plus-inch holdover trout. There is little bank fishing, but it has a good boat ramp. It is open through November.

Leland Lake (Little Quilcene): Sprawling along Highway 101 four miles north of Quilcene, 99-acre Leland Lake is Jefferson County's largest lake. It also receives the largest springtime plant of hatchery fish each spring, approximately 10,000 legal rainbows and around 300 triploids. It is very popular with bait-anglers and those who fish off the dock, but you don't see many fly-fishers. It has a boat launch.

Devils Lake: Nestled on the flanks of Mount Walker, this 12-acre forest gem was accessible by vehicle until a washout took out the road about a mile from the lake. In 2002, the DNR designated the lake and surrounding forest and wetlands a Natural Resource Conservation Area, and there are no plans to fix the road. So if you want to fish Devils Lake, you will have to hike. This is one of the few lakes in the area that contains rainbow, cutthroat and brookies.

Lena Lake (Hamma Hamma): The three-mile trail (1,150 feet elevation gain) to this 55-acre montane zone lake sees as much foot traffic as a golf fairway, and on sunny holiday weekends 50 or more cars may be parked at the Forest Service's Lena Lake trailhead. Nonetheless, it can provide good trout fishing once it warms up in late spring. It has been planted since the 1930s with everything from brook trout to rainbow to cutthroat. The trailhead is on FR 25, which is paved the entire eight miles from Highway 101. Campsites are available at the lake and at the Lena Creek Campground at the trailhead.

Elk Lakes (Hamma Hamma): These two swampy lakes are situated at around 1,100 feet at the base of Jefferson Ridge, approximately eight miles from Highway 101 off FR 24 and 2401. At high water, the lakes seem to merge, but during late summer they shrink into approximately six-acre (lower) and three-acre (upper) lakes. They have been planted with a variety of species over the years, but cutthroat and brook trout are available today. The shoreline is brushy, and float tubes are a good idea if there is enough water.

Jefferson Lakes (Hamma Hamma): The Jefferson Lakes are located at 1,800 feet about three miles past the Elk Lakes on FR 2401. The upper lake is three acres and the lower is 10 acres. They too have a tendency to shrink in late summer, and cutthroat and some eastern brooks are available.

Melbourne Lake (Eagle Cr.): Located southwest of Eldon, this 34-acre lake was used as a rearing pond in the 1930s and '40s, but self-sustaining cutthroat are the targets today. It turns out fair numbers of fish larger than 12 inches, and they tend to be fat and deep-bodied. Forest Road 24 and Melbourne Lake Road provide access, and the DNR operates a small campground between the late April opener and September 15, after which the road closes.

Osborne Lakes (Lilliwaup Cr.): These two crescent-shaped lakes cover four and two acres and are located approximately 2/3 of a mile south of Melbourne Lakes. The State plants a few hundred adult rainbow, and they provide early season angling. The Melbourne Lake Road provides access when it is open.

Price Lake (Lilliwaup): Shallow and full of insect-producing weedbeds, 61-acre Price Lake is the most famous trout lake in the Hood Canal basin. It had a popular fishing camp from the late 1920s through the 1950s, and cutthroat and eastern brook trout to five pounds were taken. The lake doesn't produce many big trout today, but it's still a lovely place to fish during spring and fall. There is no development or shoreline access, and the only way to fish it is to lug a float tube or raft down a steep quarter-mile trail. The trail is located on the 1,100 Road, which forks off the 1000 Road near Lake Cushman State Park. The launch is muddy and full of roots. Also be on the watch for submerged snags, which are common in the lake. Price Lake has scuds and robust insect populations.

Lake Cushman (North Fork Skokomish): Lake Cushman is only about two miles from Price Lake, but the atmosphere and fishing techniques could hardly be more different.

Instead of float tubes, beefy power boats are standard; and instead of flies that imitate insects or tiny crustaceans, most anglers on Lake Cushman troll plugs or spoons that suggest baitfish. This makes sense on a lake with more than 4,000 surface acres of water and is more than seven miles long. The lake is also subject to fierce downslope winds from the North Fork Skokomish, which can swamp a float tube or canoe. But more fly-fishers should give the reservoir's cutthroat a shot. The state releases in excess of 23,000 cutthroat fry annually, and 10- to 15-inch cutthroat are often taken from the flooded timber at the north end of the lake and from coves and creek mouths. Cushman also contains kokanee and landlocked chinook salmon, and salmon fry and fingerlings provide a rich, year-round forage base for larger cutthroat. The reservoir is extremely clear, and long fine leaders are often necessary. The water level fluctuates seasonally, and is usually lowest in late fall and winter. Bull trout also inhabit the lake, but are listed under the ESA and may not be pursued. In addition to Lake Cushman State Park and the Lake Cushman Resort, camping is available at the boat-in Deer Meadow and Dry Creek camps. Kokanee Lake, a smaller impoundment downstream of Cushman, is primarily a kokanee-trolling destination.

Spider Lake: A long, narrow lake at the head of Cedar Creek, it has been stocked continuously since the 1930s. Traditionally turned out nice brookies and cutthroat, but the planting focus has been on cutthroat recently. A beautiful forest lake with a trail around it.

Pine Lake: Located at the head of Pine Creek, seven-acre Pine Lake has received rainbow, cutthrout and eastern brook in the past. The trailhead begins off FR Road 2361-21 and it is three miles to the lake.

Section 4
Chehalis/Grays Harbor

Fly originated by Emil Faulk; tied by Doug Rose.

Faulk Special

Hook: Wet fly, 6-14
Tail: Hackle fibers, red
Body: Orange wool
Hackle: Four turns medium gold rope
Hackle: Red
Wing/Head: Bucktail, with head forward like Elk Hair Caddis

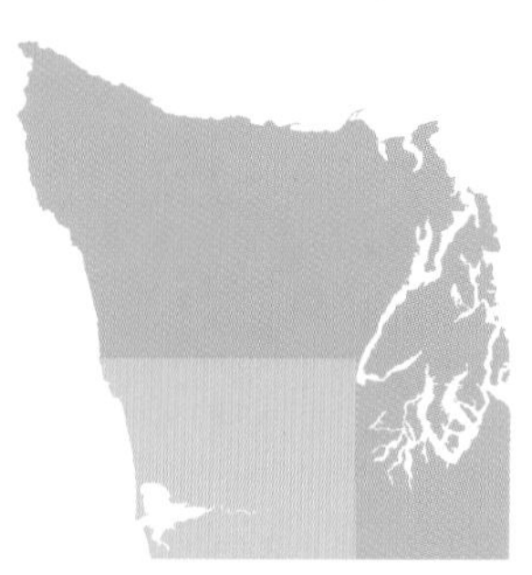

MAP C: Chehalis/Grays Harbor

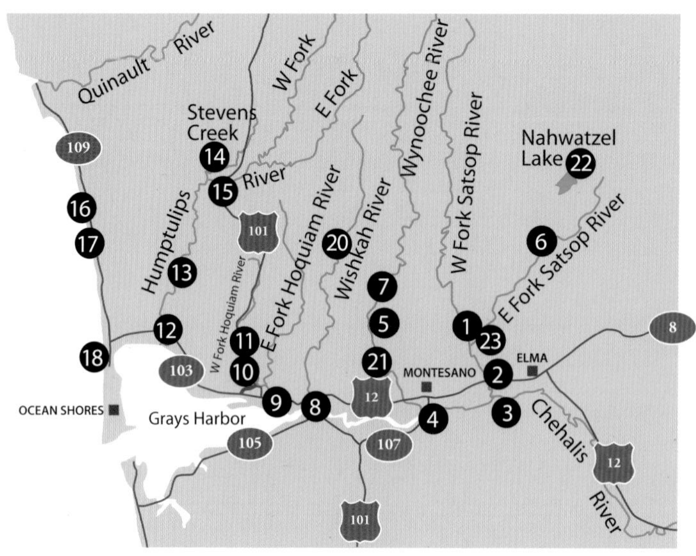

1. West Branch ramp
2. Highway 12 boat ramp
3. Porter Bridge boat ramp
4. South Monte boat ramp (the take-out for the lower drift, the South Monte ramp is located downstream of Highway 12)
5. Crossover ramp
6. Bingham Creek Hatchery
7. White Bridge ramp
8. Wishkah River takeout
9. Levee and 9th Street boat ramp
10. River access (no trailers)
11. River access (no trailers)
12. WDFW boat ramp
13. Boat ramp
14. Stevens Creek Hatchery
15. Boat ramp
16. Pacific Beach State Park access
17. Griffith-Priday State Park access
18. Ocean City State Park
19. East Fork Humptulips boat ramp
20. Wishkah River boat ramp
21. Black Creek ramp
22. Nahwatzel Lake
23. Schafer State Park and ramp

Chapter Thirteen

Satsop Sloughs and Silvers

The Highway 112 boat ramp on the Satsop River.

We launched the old aluminum driftboat, a serviceable Clackacraft, at the Highway 12 Bridge over the Satsop, a couple of miles west of Elma. It was late October, and coho should have been in the river. But we had yet another dry summer, with a record-setting lack of rain. All of the Olympic Peninsula rivers were as low as I had ever seen them, and people who have lived here a lot longer than I have said the same thing. Coho that should have provided fine sport at Pillar Point and Point Wilson weeks ago were still in the ocean, and the silver run to the West End rivers was late too. I had even been forced to cancel cutthroat trips on the Hoko because there just wasn't any water.

Actually, my friends, Joe Uhlman and Joe Aldrich, and I were fishing for cutthroat. The Satsop was historically a superb sea-run stream, and in his 1979 classic book *Sea-Run* Les Johnson said that he thought it turned out the largest cutthroat in the Gray's Harbor region. We figured if we were going to see cutthroat anywhere it would be on the lower Satsop. The first legs of a Satsop cutthroat's freshwater migration, after all, are through Grays Harbor and the lower, tidal Chehalis—places that always have plenty of water. The same applies for coho, and we had 8-weights in the boat in case we saw any heavy boils or swirls.

As always happens when I am in the southern Olympics, I was surprised by how different it looks than other parts of the peninsula. The lower reaches of the Satsop are much flatter, with long sweeps of unobstructed horizon. There are fewer trees, and the Olympic foothills, smoky blue in the autumn haze, seemed a long way away. Even though you are only a few dozen miles from the Pacific Ocean, there isn't much sense that you are in a coastal area either. It feels inland, like the upper Snoqualmie Valley or southwest

Fishing for coho on a Chehalis River tributary.

Washington. The land seems more worked over and worn down, as though you could drive a tractor across it.

We didn't catch very many cutthroat that day and didn't see any coho until we were within hailing distance of the Chehalis. I still had a good time. I spend a lot of time on rivers, and a slow day here and there isn't a big deal. It probably has something to do with my getting older and calmer, but it seems clear to me that "unproductive" days and "bad" days are entirely different things. Bad days are nearly always the result of other people. Unproductive days can be a lot of fun, and I always feel like I learn something.

One of the first things I learned that day was that there are resident rainbows in the Satsop. As we drifted downstream, fanning casts to the deep slots and snags along the bank, Joe Aldrich told me that he targets them during summer. "They're in the riffles like anywhere else," he said. Joe wasn't sure if they were a true population of resident rainbows or residualized hatchery steelhead, but he said that he takes them to 14 inches and that 10 to 12 inches is average. Joe has analyzed the larvae and pupae in the river and created *Rhyacophilla* and *Hydropsyche* patterns that take fish readily in the broken water.

Not long after that, casting straight downstream with a black Reverse Spider, I hooked into what I thought was a cutthroat, although the water was a little streamier than I typically associate with cutts. It jumped repeatedly, though, and when I brought it up alongside the boat it was an 8-inch rainbow. Some smolts are that big, but this fish was too colored-up to be on its way to the salt. I suppose it could have been a hatchery steelhead plant that simply found the river to its liking. But it may very well have been a resident rainbow. There are a lot of mysteries in Olympic Peninsula rivers.

By far the most interesting discovery I made that day was about the big sloughs on the Satsop and other lower Chehalis River tributaries. As we floated, Joe Uhlman kept saying he was looking for a slough on the right bank. He said that he fished it all the time until the road into it washed out.

"You actually fish in the sloughs?" I asked.

"Sure," Joe said. "They can be great."

"What for?"

"Coho and chum," Joe Aldrich said.

That was intriguing, because few fly-fishers bother with sloughs on the West End or along the strait or Hood Canal. You see coho in sloughs on the middle and lower Hoh and

Queets, and chum in the Duckabush and Dosewallips. But these are usually old, spawned-out fish, waiting to die. That's not what the two Joes were talking about. They take bright fish in sloughs, silvers in October and chum in November.

"The fish hold in them," Joe Uhlman explained.

That reminded me of Les Johnson writing about catching cutthroat in Grays Harbor and Willapa Bay sloughs when he was young. I lived on a Hood Canal slough for five years and never saw a cutthroat in it, and my friend, Ron Hirschi, who grew up along Hood Canal, has never caught a cutt in one. Something is clearly different about the Satsop River sloughs and those of the other large rivers that drain the south flanks of the Olympics. I got my first glimmer of the difference a short time later.

"It's around here someplace," Joe Uhlman said. Then, as we rounded a bend, he pointed to the right. "That's it."

It was big, stretching at least a hundred yards off the main channel and with a mouth at least 30 yards across. Despite the drought, the water was green and looked deep. Its banks were rimmed with vegetation, small alders and willows, and its channel had an abundance of snags and structure. We didn't get out and look, but I think it is at least partially spring-fed. The side-channels—abandoned river channels that capture water when the water is high—we had passed earlier had been bone dry, but the slough looked lush and green. It was a welcoming-looking place for an early-timed salmon.

Later, at the takeout near Fuller Bridge on the Chehalis, I stayed with the boat while the two Joes retrieved the trailer. As I had been all day, I was struck again by how flat the lower Satsop appears. And I thought about how glaciers tell the story of the lower Chehalis Valley just as they do the Hoh and Elwha. Approximately 15,000 years ago, a huge ice sheet blocked the mouth of the Strait of Juan de Fuca, damming the outflows of the Fraser River and all Puget Sound streams. This created an immense lake. Eventually, the lake burst and water surged west from near present-day Olympia to the coast. The torrent was three times the size of the current Columbia. It scoured the lower Chehalis Basin.

In this sort of low-gradient terrain, with its abundance of groundwater, sloughs can be large, and they can be long-lived. That distinguishes them from side channels and flood-plain ponds, which are also important for juvenile coho and chum but are smaller and transitory. The lower reaches of these rivers are also rich in springs. These perennial sources of cool water attract fish like beacons, especially during low water. During high flows, sloughs provide off-channel refuge for fish. Chum like to spawn in sloughs, and eggs in sloughs survive high water better than those in areas susceptible to flooding and scour.

The trick with fishing sloughs on the Satsop or any other lower Chehalis River tributary is finding them. Most of the land along the lower portions of these rivers is private, and it is farmland or dairy land, not timberlands with log roads. There are rough four-wheel-drive tracks that locals use to reach the river, but most of them end up on big pools, not sloughs. Basically, if you are from out of town and want to fish a slough, you need a boat. On our half-day float, we passed at least four major sloughs, sloughs large enough that a small boat could row up into them.

That isn't the way you fish them, though.

"You usually anchor up at the mouth and fish from foot," Joe Uhlman said. "The sloughs are usually surrounded by vegetation so you have to find a spot where you can cast. Usually, I would fish from the mouth of the slough, where it meets the river. But there are times when you can fish from the sides. Sometimes there is a gravel bar between the river and slough and you can fish from it. I cast up into the slough and strip the fly back. I like a fairly slow, say medium, retrieve, and I usually fish an intermediate line because some sloughs aren't very deep."

Chapter Fourteen

Canoe Country Cutthroat

Cutthroat return to Joe Creek in autumn.

Olympic Peninsula rivers aren't usually thought of as canoeing destinations. Tumbling rapidly out of the mountains, down steep watercourses salted liberally with boulder gardens, gorges and cascades—not to mention waterfalls—the upper reaches aren't safe for anything but river kayaks. The lower rivers have been the province of drift boats for a half century, and more recently jet sleds and pontoon boats have become popular. According to my friend, the late Roy Bergstrom, salvage loggers from Oregon brought the first McKenzie and Rogue type dories to the West End after the Forks Fire in 1951. Not everyone welcomed the new watercraft. "Drift boats will be the demise of our fishing," Syd Glasso told Dick Wentworth. For his part, Wentworth preferred the smaller, more maneuverable classic bayou boat, the pirogue, which let him navigate creeks, low summer flows and is easily portaged.

Of course, the Olympic Peninsula's Indians traveled both the rivers and the oceans in canoes, and they were widely regarded as some of the most skillful paddlers in the world. The coastal tribes stuck with their hand-carved boats long after gasoline engines became common. When Roderick Haig-Brown fished the lower Quinault River in the 1950s, he fished from a dugout canoe with an 18-horsepower Evinrude. "It was very beautiful," he wrote in a 1988 *Sports Illustrated* article,". . . Nootka pattern, flat-bottomed, with straight flaring sides, vertical stern and high prow, over 27 feet long and about 42 inches wide, black and slender and graceful, yet strong and stable, perfectly adapted for river work."

I don't know if you can still book a float in a dugout on the lower Quinault, but the best places to paddle your own canoe on the Olympic Peninsula today are the rivers of its southern flank. Larger rivers like the Satsop and Humptulips have good flatwater canoeing reaches in their lower ends, and the Hoquiam, Wishkah and East Fork of the Satsop have smaller more intimate water to explore.

"In my younger days as an Aberdeen kid, we fished the Humptulips, Wishkah, Hoquiam and other rivers and creeks in the fall for what we called bluebacks," said Les Johnson, author of *Fly-Fishing for Coastal Cutthroat Trout* and other Northwest fly-fishing classics. "These were coastal (sea-run) cutthroat newly returned from the salt, usually in August and September. It was popular in those days to fish at night using bullheads (immature sculpin 3 to 4 inches long). Some of the little local restaurants between Aberdeen and Forks offered 'Harvest Trout Breakfasts' during the blueback season."

Of all the Grays Harbor County rivers, perhaps none presents the fly-fisher with the variety of opportunity and scenery as the Hoquiam. Flowing into the Chehalis through the industrial waterfront of Hoquiam, the lower river quickly becomes rural as you move upstream. Its banks are lined with private homes and businesses for several miles, but its upper reaches penetrate timberlands and wetlands. The Hoquiam contains three forks, all of them navigable. The East Fork merges with the West Fork (considered the mainstem) at River Mile 2.4, and the Middle Fork joins the West Fork at RM 7.1 Because the gradient is so low, the tide reaches more than nine miles up the West Fork. Boat launches are available on the east and west forks, but there is no access to the middle fork.

"We fished the Hoquiam, which was a good cutthroat stream," Les Johnson, told me, "but so very brushy above tidewater that it had to be fished by boat. I never heard of anyone canoeing up the Hoquiam. We rowed a wooden boat, with two rowing stations up the Hoquiam on the incoming tide and anchored up to fish for cutthroat, which went for bullheads or worms and spinners. We would then drop downstream as the tide fell until we reached the place that we'd put in, which has long disappeared to some commercial buildings."

Although it supports coho, chum and winter steelhead, cutthroat remain the Hoquiam's principal fly-rod target. At one time, it and the other Grays Harbor streams were among the most prolific coastal cutthroat rivers on the peninsula, maybe in all of Washington. Overfishing and habitat degradation have taken their toll, and cutthroat populations have declined. But the Hoquiam and its sister rivers are still marvelous places to spend a day alternating between handling a canoe paddle and a 5-weight. Canoes let you work water that is inaccessible to bank anglers and avoided by those in more conventional watercraft, and these snaggy, brushy slack-water areas are often exactly the type of water cutthroat prefer.

I usually like to use a canoe the way most fly-fishers use drift boats—that is, I beach it and get out and wade when I want to fish. However, tidal mud and deep banks make it safer to fish most reaches of the Hoquiam from the canoe. If you have two people in the canoe, the one in the stern can paddle and the one in the bow can cast to streamside obstructions and cover. It's just like hopper fishing in Montana. If you're alone, the best strategy is to anchor-up in productive-looking cutt water.

Finally, don't get too adventurous. The Hoquiam and Wishkah and lower Satsop are relatively tame, but the upper portions of the larger rivers, including the Satsop's forks, have places that can kill you. You don't want your first glimpse of a narrow gorge or waterfall to be over the bow of your canoe.

Chapter Fifteen

Lake Nahwatzel's Cold-Weather Trout

Nahwatzel Lake is unique. Located in the upper basin of the East Fork of the Satsop, only a dozen miles from Shelton, Nahwatzel often turns out Mason County's largest "opening-day" trout, fish well over 20 inches, but the lowest success rates. Moreover, the best trout fishing on the lake, which is open year-round, occurs between late fall and late spring. If you visit it during summer, you will see more jet skis and bass fishermen than trout anglers. Despite turning out rainbow and cutthroat in excess of four pounds, the lake isn't fished heavily by trout anglers. Finally, Nahwatzel Lake is a place where a fly-fisher can basically forget about insects, because you are going to take most fish, and especially the better ones, on streamers, Woolly Buggers, leeches and crustacean patterns.

From a boat, Nahwatzel Lake doesn't look particularly special, or even very interesting. More than 100 cottages and cabins line the 249-acre lake, and the Nahwatzel Lake Resort will sell you a steak and a bottle of beer at the end of the day. There is timbered shoreline to the north, along with the weathered pilings of the sawmill that operated when the forest around the lake was logged in the 1930s. Although topographical maps show a couple of inlets, you won't notice them, and the outlet simply disappears through the marsh on the southwest corner of the lake. On a clear day, you can see the foothills of the Olympics to the north.

The things that make Nahwatzel Lake unique, that distinguish it from other lowland, forested lakes on the Olympic Peninsula, all occur beneath its surface. The most important is that it is spring fed. This maintains relatively cool water year-round, and extraordinarily clear water. Although it is relatively shallow, with a 27-foot maximum and 17-foot average depth, the lake doesn't stratify in summer, possibly a result of the west winds that are common during warm weather. As a result, there is little seasonal change in the dissolved oxygen levels between the surface and the bottom. All of this is good for trout survival, and that is probably why the WDFW plants the lake with 18,000 rainbow fry, in addition to "catchable" rainbows and cutthroat.

Although Nahwatzel has few lily pads or other surface vegetation, it contains chara beds. Chara is a subaquatic weed that is relatively rare in western Washington, but is common on lakes east of the Cascades that produce large trout. In addition to supporting abundant populations of sub-aquatic insects, chara is a favored habitat of scuds. Many Nahwatzel Lake fish have the deep-red flesh characteristic of trout that prey heavily on scuds. Moreover, adult coho from the East Fork Satsop have been able to migrate through the lake to tributary spawning grounds since the state removed an outlet screen in 1999. Juvenile coho have been observed in the lake, and I don't imagine they are completely ignored by the lake's larger trout.

Fly-fishers who spend most of their time on shallow, insect-rich lakes like Anderson Lake or Price Lake need to adjust their approach on Nahwatzel. For starters, you will be more comfortable and safer here in a boat than a float tube. Nahwatzel is notorious for its west wind, which often kicks up during the warm part of the day. The water is also cold during late autumn, winter and early spring, when most trout anglers visit the lake, and you will fish longer and more effectively if you are dry and warm. Because most of the trout action takes place before or after the bulk of its insect hatches, the most productive patterns are streamers and scud imitations. Large Woolly Buggers and Seal Buggers in black, brown and chartreuse are good, and a size 6 or 4 Mickey Finn is a surprisingly good juvenile coho pattern.

Nahwatzel's exceptionally clear water is at its absolute most transparent during the winter, and I believe a clear or camo intermediate line is your best bet, even if you need to give it extra time to sink. Fluorocarbon leaders and tippets, which are tough and nearly invisible, are also worth the expense. Slow retrieves are always preferable in cold water, and it is often a good idea to let a fly rest for a time on the bottom, then strip it sharply.

Rivers

Satsop River: The mainstem Satsop and its East, Decker, Middle and West forks (Map C1) drain the largest watershed on the north bank of the Chehalis, more than 300 square miles. But its headwaters don't penetrate the southern Olympics' high ridges and peaks, and the basin is dominated by low-gradient feeder creeks, wetlands, swamps and springs. This stable, rain-fed habitat is ideal for coho, and the Satsop was originally one of the most productive silver systems in the Northwest. Coho ran from October into January and 20-pounders were taken every year. The Satsop was also heralded for its large sea-run cutthroat. Both coho and cutthroat numbers have declined, but cutthrout still provide fine sport in September and anglers take several thousand silvers between October and January. Chum appear in late October and run into December, and winter steelhead return from December into March, with larger fish more common later in the season. The Washington record chum, a 25-pounder, is a Satsop fish. Boats are the most efficient way to fish the mainstem, and ramps are located at Schafer State Park, the Highway 12 bridge (Map C2) and at the Fuller Bridge (Map C3) takeout on the Chehalis (you row upstream from the Satsop to the ramp).

Wynoochee River: Rising up in Olympic National Park, the Wynoochee River presents an entirely different aspect than the Satsop. It drops from the high country to the Chehalis down a more or less straight channel, through several canyons and gorges, and it doesn't have any major tributaries. It is the only Chehalis River tributary with a large run of hatchery summer steelhead. The most popular drift is from the White Bridge ramp (Map C7) down to the Lower Monte takeout near Montesano (Map C4). Before the introduction of Skamania-stock summer fish in the 1980s, the Wynoochee was best known as a winter steelheading destination and turned out 20-plus-pound natives. Most winter fish caught today are hatchery steelhead. Whether it's winter or summer, word gets around quickly when steelhead are available, and armadas of drift boats and sleds can make for miserable fly-fishing. Moreover, bank access is extremely limited as a result of private property, virtually all of it posted. The best strategy for wading anglers is to fish above or below the Crossover (Map C5), White Bridge and 7400 Line Bridge boat ramps. Since the construction of the Wynoochee Dam, the state has transported adult steelhead, coho and, more recently, chinook above Wynoochee Reservoir. Not that many people pursue them, but you can fish for winter steelhead above the lake.

Wishkah River: The Wishkah may not provide the best fly-fishing on the Olympic Peninsula but it is the only river mentioned in the title of a best-selling record album. *From the Muddy Banks of the Wishkah* is the title of Nirvana's last live album, and according to legend, band member and Aberdeen native Kurt Cobain slept under the Wishkah Bridge when he dropped out of high school. The lower, tidal end of the Wishkah flows into the Chehalis less than a mile above its confluence with Grays Harbor. It contains sea-run cutthroat, winter steelhead, fall chinook, coho and chum. The salmon regulations are complex and anglers should carefully read the WDFW pamphlet. Long Live the Kings has operated a hatchery on the river since the late 1980s and releases chinook and coho. In recent years, winter steelhead have been available through February under standard regulations, but under catch-and-release and selective fishery regulations in March. All wild cutthroat must be released. The upper mainstem and its East Fork and West Fork close at the end of October. Ramps on the Wishkah Road approximately five miles north of Aberdeen and on the Chehalis, across from the Wishkah's mouth (Map C8), provide access for boats and canoes.

Hoquiam River: The Hoquiam and its east, middle and west forks present various faces to anglers. Its mouth in Aberdeen is industrial, and the lower mainstem is primarily residential and commercial. However, the remainder of the Hoquiam's 98-square-mile watershed is largely timber company land, with extensive wetlands, and much of it is inaccessible other than by boat. A large reach of the upper West Fork flows through the city of Hoquiam watershed, where public access is prohibited. Salmon are available on the mainstem and lower portion of the west and east forks during October and November, and winter steelhead are open through March under selective gear regulations. Cutthroat appear with autumn freshets and anglers take them into early winter. There is very limited bank access but launches at Rayonier Point in Hoquiam, at Fairview Acres (RM 5) on the West Fork, and off the East Fork Hoquiam Road five miles upstream of Highway 101 (RM 4), provide boat access. (Map C9, C10) There is no foot access to the Middle Fork.

Humptulips River: At one time, the Humptulips was the most celebrated river on the Washington coast. It routinely turned out enormous numbers of coho, chinook to 50 pounds, wild summer steelhead, and, for many years, the State's record winter steelhead, a 25-pounder. Sea-run cutthroat were especially abundant, and "night fishing" with bonfires under bridges produced thousands of fish. The blush has definitely come off the Humptulips over the last few decades, but hatchery chinook, coho, chum and winter steelhead sustain popular fisheries on the mainstem below Highway 101. Recent measures to protect wild chinook have included September and early October closures, so it is important to consult the current regulations pamphlet. Wild Humptulips chum are considered a healthy stock, as are its coho, which spawn in more than 60 tributaries. As on the Satsop, a significant component of its wild coho run doesn't appear until December. Boats are the best way to fish the Humptulips mainstem, and ramps are located at convenient intervals downstream of the Highway 101. (Map C12, C13, C14, C16) Bank access is available at the hatchery, but fly-fishers will have more fun near the Highway 101 bridge and in the east and west forks. The tidewater reaches of the lower Humptulips have great potential for fly-fishers willing to explore in a boat.

Copalis River: Approximately 95 percent of the Copalis River drainage is private land and most of it is managed as industrial timberlands. However, Griffith-Priday Ocean State Park (day-use only) provides access to 9,950 feet of the lower and tidal reaches of the river, as well as 8,316 acres of adjacent saltwater beach. Coho, winter steelhead and sea-run cutthroat provide the sport. Anglers occasionally catch migratory bull trout from the glacial rivers to the north, but they are listed under the ESA and must be released immediately. Coho season runs through January, and steelhead may be pursued through February.

Joe Creek: Joe Creek flows into the ocean through the community of Pacific Beach. Sea-run cutthroat and hatchery coho are the main targets, and salmon season typically runs through November. Access to the mouth is available at Pacific Beach State Park.

Moclips River: The majority of the mainstem Moclips and its north fork lie within the Quinault Indian Reservation, but anglers can find some access downstream. Sea-run cutthroat and winter steelhead are the attractions, and the river remains open through February. Although they must be released immediately, bull trout dip into the lower end, presumably to feed. The mouth of the river flows through a wide sandy beach, and is considered the northern boundary of the WDFW's "Mocrocks Beach" segment of the coast.

Lakes

Nahawtzel Lake (Satsop): On the Olympic Peninsula, fry plants are a tip that a lake is productive and that there is considerable carry-over from season to season. At first glance, 268-acre Nahwatzel Lake doesn't seem to fill that bill. It is surrounded by cabins and even has a resort, and most of the anglers that fish it are after bass. But it turns out good numbers of rainbow and cutthroat to 18 inches, and fish to four pounds are taken. The best trout fishing occurs in early spring or from October through early winter, and Woolly Buggers and leeches account for many of the larger trout. Located 11 miles west of Shelton, off the Shelton-Matlock Road, Nahwatzel has a WDFW boat launch and is planted with adult rainbow and cutthroat in addition to fry.

Stump Lake (Chehalis): Littered with stumps and snags, 23-acre Stump Lake near Elma contains some cutthroat and brook trout but is stocked with around 2,000 legal rainbows annually. It is a popular float-tube lake, and is accessible from the Cloquallum and Stump Lake roads. It has a rough boat ramp.

Lake Sylvia (Wynoochee): Located within Lake Sylvia State Park, Lake Sylvia is actually a small (31-acre) reservoir on Sylvia Creek. It is stocked with legal rainbows, as well as triploids and large broodstock trout. It's popular with families and youngsters camping in the park, but local fly-fishers are drawn by the potential for large fish. Lake Sylvia is most productive early in the season and again in early autumn.

Aberdeen Lake: As many as 9,000 hatchery rainbow, as well as nearly 200 triploids, are released in this 64-acre reservoir. Fishing is best in spring for catchable plants and triploids to several pounds, and for holdovers to 15 inches during autumn. It is located just east of Aberdeen and has a launch and bank access.

Failor Lake (Humptulips): This lake was formed by a dam on Deep Creek, a tributary to the Humptulips. It is approximately nine miles north of Hoquiam and is usually around 60 acres. It is popular with small-boat anglers during the early season, when it receives adult rainbows and triploids. It was named for Walter Failor, who operated Failor's Sporting Goods in Aberdeen for years and was a mayor of Aberdeen.

Satsop Lakes: These five lakes are scattered along the upper West Fork of the Satsop, a few miles northeast of Grisdale. They have all been planted in the past. Currently, Lakes Number One and Two contain cutthroat and eastern brook. Lake 2 has scuds.

Section 5

The Coast, The Strait, The Canal

Fly originated and tied by Jeffrey Delia.

Delia's Conehead Squid

Hook: TMK 5263 BL 10
Tail: Cream marabou
Body: Ice chenille, medium, clear
Cone Head: Gold, small or medium

Chapter Sixteen

Indian Island Cutthroat

The author fishing Indian Island during late fall.

Winter may very well be my favorite time to fish Indian Island, the five-mile-long island tucked between the east shore of the Quimper Peninsula and Marrowstone Island. My angling journals show that I take more fish in spring and early fall. But the fact that I can catch saltwater cutthroat at all in winter, not to mention on a reasonably regular basis, puts the island in a league by itself. What's a reasonably regular basis? Well, I think two fish for about four hours of fishing is a good winter day. Even one saltwater cutthroat is a gift on a glum winter day, as far as I'm concerned. They're all wild, after all.

The U.S. Navy controls most of Indian Island, and they won't let you on it. Their rent-a-soldiers even chase you away if you get too close to the beach in a boat. But Jefferson County administers the portion of the island south of State Route 116 as county park and public beach. This gives fly-fishers access to more than two miles of shoreline. It includes long stretches of gravel and cobble beach, oyster bars and clam beds, two lagoons, salt marsh, sand spits, a rocky point, and near-shore eelgrass flats. It's classic sea-run cutthroat water, some of the finest I know.

Let me repeat: You definitely catch fewer cutthroat in salt water during winter, but there are usually a few fish around Indian Island and other protected areas of the leeward Olympics. The rivers and creeks of Admiralty Inlet, northern Hood Canal, and the eastern Strait of Juan de Fuca nearly

Jeffrey Delia with a winter cutthroat in northern Hood Canal.

always experience low flows in autumn. Cutthroat native to these streams tend to remain in tidewater until the streams rise, often late December or January. Other cutthroat simply seem to prefer the region's food-rich bays and inlets to the hard-scrabble life of creeks. These fish delay their spawning runs until late winter or spring and drop back down to tidewater quickly. Some cutthroat also seem to skip their freshwater run entirely from time to time.

Jeffrey Delia, who created the incredibly effective Delia's Conehead Squid and who has fished for Hood Canal cutthroat for 30 years, told me that December is one of his best months. I caught my largest cutthroat last year on December 5, during a sharp cold spell after days of rain. Fishing does seem to taper off in late January and February. That is probably when the fish that have lingered in tidewater finally get around to spawning. But the largest cutthroat that Ron Hirschi ever saw taken on a fly rod was a February fish from Hood Canal. It was 24 1/2 inches long and weighed more than 4 pounds. Incredibly, a friend of Ron's caught it on his first saltwater cutthroat fishing trip. They were in canoes and the wind was blowing, the fish hit a scarlet Bucktail.

I fished Indian Island in early December last year, after the wettest November on record. The West End rivers had been out for weeks, and I had been blown off Indian Island duck hunting earlier in the week. It takes a lot to make me throw in the towel on duck hunting, but I figured it was time to go when I turned around and saw a picnic table bobbing in eye-level swells ten feet behind my blind. No matter how heavy the wind or waves, however, the waters around Indian Island always settle down much faster than a steelhead river. Two days later, the water was flat and calm. Brant pecked eelgrass in the shallows and herons waded the lagoons.

There are two prime places to fish the Indian Island shoreline—Government Cut and the flat. Known locally as "the cut"—and as Portage Canal on charts—Government Cut is the half-mile-long channel between Port Townsend Bay and Oak Bay. It is the body of water you cross on the bridge between the mainland and Indian Island. Historically, it was more of a tidal marsh than a channel, and the Chimacum Indians poled across it in canoes. A ferry provided access to the island after the cut was dredged and deepened, and you can still see the pilings from the ferry landing to the northwest of the bridge.

The flat is the large tide flat adjacent to the south end of Government Cut, east of the jetty. A large tidal lagoon, known locally as "stinky pond," drains into the flat from the east. The lagoon and most of the south end of the flat are bordered by a sand spit. At low tide, the terminal end of the spit looks like a four-foot berm, but it is completely submerged at high water. The flat itself is muddy sand with gravel, and hosts a dizzying array of intertidal creatures. On a good minus clam tide, you see sand dollars and polychaete worm burrows, manila clams and blue mussels and thousands of shore crabs.

Both the cut and the flat turn out fish during winter but I began that December morning at the cut, as I nearly always do. Because of the huge volume of water flowing through it and the four daily tide turns, the cut nearly always has moving water. Slack tides are short, and even then there is usually some current. As a result, the most productive way to fish it is the same way you would for sea-run cutthroat in a stream in autumn. You cast across and down current, let the fly swing downstream, then strip it back. Sometimes you strip on the swing, sometimes you let the current work the fly. But you always retrieve against the current.

By the way, don't assume all incoming tides at the cut flow from north to south—that is from Port Townsend Bay, which is closer to the ocean, toward Oak Bay—and vice versa on ebbing tides. Sometimes the current flows, occasionally even strongly flows, contrary to what makes sense. Ben Porter, one of the people I regularly guide, told me that you encounter the same thing around Bainbridge Island, where it is occasionally possible to paddle all the way around the island with the current. I suppose it's because of tidal bores of something that I wouldn't understand if they were explained to me. I always just pick up a piece of driftwood and throw it ten feet into the water and see which way it drifts.

It was still legal to keep saltwater cutthroat during the 1970s.

Last December, I tied on a brown-over-cream variation of a Clouser Minnow that Kurt Beardslee, Washington Trout's executive director, had shown me a couple of years earlier. It's tied with badger and brown-phase black bear fur. I caught my largest saltwater cutthroat on it two years ago, an 18-plus-inch bruiser on Dabob Bay. I fished it on a basic 9-foot 3X leader, and my standard saltwater cutthroat line, a Cortland camo intermediate. I began casting at the bottom of the path that leads from the Lions Club Park to the beach. A cluster of washing-machine-sized boulders are scattered just offshore, and cutthroat often hang downtide of them and in the seams they create. I began casting from shore, and my first casts were inside the rocks, not more than 20 feet from the shell line.

That day began a lot faster than most winter cutthroat trips. I got a nice sharp hit on about my fifth swing. It was a strong 12-incher, and it jumped three times and threw the fly. I had another tap a couple minutes later, but missed it. Then I felt a slow pull. I've been fishing saltwater cutthroat for a long time and know enough to keep stripping when you feel fish. Moments later, I felt another tentative tug and, finally, a hard-pulling yank. I struck and stripped line. It never jumped. Instead, it thrashed and rolled and fought deeply around the rocks. I didn't get a good look at it until I brought it to hand. It had a purplish smudge on its gill plates, as winter fish commonly do, and was deep-bodied, with a birdshot splatter of black spots over tarnished silver flanks. It was an honest 15 inches.

Actually, I often do a little better at the flat during winter. The highest tides of the day occur during daytime in winter. That means that water pushing down the cut from Admiralty Inlet (if the tide is normal) spills across the inside of the jetty and floods the flat and lagoon. If it is a morning tide, the flat and lagoon will begin to drain at midday or during the afternoon. On a nice slow run-out, cutthroat will often feed aggressively as amphipods and shrimp and sculpins drain out of the lagoon and across the flat. When the tide is making and the lagoon is low, fish seem to hang along the western edge of the flat. You take them from the slicks between the cut and the jetty and the end of the spit.

Although winter may be my favorite season at Indian Island, I fish it year-round. During early spring, columns of chum salmon fry move up the inside edge of the cut's eelgrass. I catch cutthroat with my Keta Rose pattern and Bob Triggs does just as well on his Chum Baby, although the two flies look nothing alike. Port Townsend Bay, Oak Bay and Government Cut also support strong populations of sand lance, surf smelt and herring, and cutts work them hard in late spring and early summer. Jim Kerr's polychaete imitation, the Jim Dandy, is an excellent pattern year-round, while the shimmering translucent body and tan marabou tail of Jeffrey Delia's Conehead Squid suggests everything from larval fish to amphipods to juvenile shrimp and, oh yeah, squid.

Chapter Seventeen

Swiftsure Coho

My friend, Jay Brevik, came up the perfect summary of our day on Swiftsure Bank before we had even caught a salmon. "I've never seen anything like this," he said.

It was the first day of September, and we were fishing with our friend, Chris Bellows, who operated a fly-fishing charter out of Neah Bay at the time. We had just located a huge patch of krill. Thousands upon thousands, probably millions, of the orange, mayfly-sized crustaceans ranged from just beneath the surface to as deep as we could see. Gulls and fulmars and shearwaters worked them frantically from above, and schools of fast-moving mackerel chomped through them from below. The fish we were pursuing, coho salmon, slashed along the edges of the swarm, their dorsal fins occasionally breaking the surface.

Straddling the Canadian/US border approximately 15 miles northwest of Neah Bay, Swiftsure Bank is a 20-square-mile submarine plateau at the junction of the Strait of Juan de Fuca and the Pacific Ocean. During September, coho are the salmon you are most likely to encounter on Swiftsure. Because they are closer to sexual maturity than the silvers that entered the strait in July and August, the males often display the enlarged kype that gives them their nickname—"hooknose". The added feeding time at sea also produces larger fish, with many in the 10-plus-pound range, and a few push the 20-pound mark.

Chris turned off the engine and Jay picked up his 8-weight. "Cast along the outside of the bait and strip it back as fast as you can, like I showed you."

Jay hauled back and shot the 24-foot intermediate head. He tucked the rod under his arm and stripped quickly, hand-over-hand. He didn't connect on his first few casts, but eventually a luminescent blue-green shape appeared behind the fly. It was only about 30 feet from the boat.

"Keep stripping," Chris said.

Suddenly, the fish darted forward and snatched the fly. Jay struck and grabbed the rod with both hands. The coho whirled and streaked away from the boat. It made several runs, but eventually Jay worked it back to the boat. We could see that its dorsal fin was intact. That meant that it was a wild fish, and only fin-clipped hatchery fish could be kept in the area we were fishing. Chris removed the fly and the salmon swam away. It was about an 8-pounder.

On my previous trips with Chris, when rough seas had kept us closer to shore, we fished high-density sinking heads, and had retrieved them with a slower, single-handed strip. It was very effective when the coho were working baitfish like herring. But Chris had discovered that the intermediate line is all you need when the salmon are feeding on krill near the surface. Moreover, the intermediate is better at keeping the fly away from the mackerel, which tend to feed slightly deeper. The faster retrieve also produces more coho than mackerel.

Why fish the Clouser Minnow, a baitfish pattern, when the salmon were feeding on much smaller crustaceans? "They just catch more fish," Chris said, with a shrug. The presence of a larger, faster silhouette among the thousands of krill, he theorized, may simply do a better job of catching the eye of a coho.

Jay and I took turns casting after that. We each caught several coho within an hour of locating the bait. They ranged from 6 to 10 pounds, and most of them were wild. We also caught our first mackerel. These were Pacific mackerel, not the foot-long jack mackerel that move into the north Pacific during El Niño years. They averaged a couple of pounds, and a few were close to five. When you first hooked one, it was hard to tell if it was a salmon or mackerel.

I eventually connected with a larger fish. It streaked up behind the fly, then dropped back. Then it reappeared. I could see its white mouth open as it moved on the fly. It missed.

"Keep it coming," Chris and Jay said, simultaneously.

It took the fly within a rod length of the boat, then raced away. It peeled line effortlessly and was into the reel's bright orange backing before I could respond. Then it jumped. It was a heavy, ponderous jump, and I could see that it was well over ten pounds. It had the classic football shape of a large wild coho.

"Take it easy," Chris said. "That's a nice one."

Eventually, I brought it within sight of the boat, but it ran again. I had my second look at the backing. Fortunately, the knots were strong, and the hook hold was secure. After its two long runs, it fought off the stern, moving between port and starboard. It was obviously wearing down.

Chris picked up the net. "Don't reel any more," he said. "Just lead it to me."

I wasn't particularly surprised when the fish dashed off again. I worked it back to the starboard side a few minutes later, and Chris slipped the net beneath it. It was even bigger than I had thought, with the classic hook-nose of a large, late-season male. But it was still as luminous as river water.

"It's 13 or 14 pounds," he said. "And it's wild. Let's get the hook out."

"That's the biggest coho I've caught on a fly," I said.

Chris grinned broadly, "That's what I like to hear."

Chapter Eighteen

Hood Canal Chum

Casting into the autumn gloom for chum salmon.

One late November day a few years ago, Jay Brevik and I launched his boat at the Tacoma PUD ramp north of Potlatch. We loaded it with shotguns and 5-weights and 8-weights, and then headed east, down the "great bend" toward the Tahuya and Union rivers. Our plan was pretty amorphous, but if someone had asked, we would probably have said that we were going to look for ducks and sea-run cutthroat and chum salmon. In other words, we weren't going to do any of these things very seriously or very well, but were, rather, in the mood to roam around in a boat and look things over. We saw chum off Belfair State Park but didn't catch any, and we cast at the mouth of the Tahuya for cutthroat but didn't see or catch any of them either. The mallards at the mouth of Rendsland's Creek wouldn't come anywhere near the boat. We decided to head back across the canal and check things out at the mouth of the WDFW's Finch Creek Hatchery.

Neither of us had ever seen the infamous CHUM FRENZY that takes place there each November when tens of thousands of hatchery chum return to the hatchery. True to its reputation, chum were everywhere. They rolled and slashed and jumped. There weren't hundreds, there were thousands. Even though it was a weekday, at least 60 people were wading and casting, and a few float-tubes bobbed around the periphery of the fishing area. About a dozen power boats worked the outside of the fish. They would follow schools of chum until the fish scattered, then motor back uptide and try again. I don't think it is putting too fine a point on it to say that some of the folks in the boats were pretty accomplished at making snagging look like fishing.

I much prefer to fly-fish for chum the way I did when my wife and I lived on a northern Hood Canal salt marsh. The salt marsh is cut by several jump-over tidal guts and is bordered on the north and south by larger, deeper sloughs. The south slough has a spring at its source, and retains a trickle of water even during summer. The guts and blind slough go dry on big low tides, then fill again as the tide makes. The salt marsh, as they all are, is as flat as a gridle and has a thatch-like cover of pickleweed and saltgrass, fleshy jaumea and sedges. The Dosewallips elk herd drifted by from time to time, and when you had a big Solstice tide that coincided with heavy rain, salt water would reach all the way to our trailer.

A narrow bit of gravel beach is the boundary between the marsh and an immense tide flat. On a big low tide, the mud extends so far into the canal that you can hardly see the green channel marker that identifies water safe enough for large boats. It is the sort of beach that cutthroat seem to go out of their way to avoid, but chum salmon think the mud flats are just fine. Summer chum, which are currently listed as "threatened" under the ESA, appear as early as August. Wild and hatchery fall chum arrive with the November rain, and they are much more abundant and are considered healthy. The larger Hood Canal rivers—the Skokomish, Hamma Hamma, Duckabush, Dosewallips and Quilcene—also host much smaller wild runs of late chum. I would see them in early December, about the time the brant and scaup showed up.

I had two driftwood blinds set up on the beach, and nearly every winter morning my yellow Labrador, Lily, and I would sit in them and try to decoy widgeon and mallards and pintail. Each December, usually early in the month and on an incoming tide, I would notice the first late chum. I would often become aware of them as they swam through the anchor lines of my decoys and set the blocks to fluttering. I would see schools of a dozen or so every morning for a few weeks. They were amazingly spooky in the shallow water. Sometimes the decoys alarmed them and they would scatter, trailing torpedo wakes. Other times they massed in small circles, boiling the water, and suddenly for no reason I could discern, they'd flash off in different directions.

I never bothered fishing for the chum until I began to see them consistently. Then I'd string my old fiberglass 8-weight and a heavy Seamaster reel with a Rio Coldwater Intermediate. I favored flies with bead-chain eyes like Comets, and about two-thirds of them were chartreuse, the rest hot pink. If I saw salmon and no birds were flying, I would unload the double-barrel and cast. I would wade up to my calves, cast as far as I could, and let the tide and current swing the line back toward shore. I stripped the line slowly once in a while, but I didn't do it fast because I didn't want to snag a fish. I also avoided the mouth of the slough, because the chum ganged up there, and it was easy to snag them.

It usually took a week or two to catch a fish that way. I would leave a little plastic fly box in a crook of the madrona limb in my duck blind, and prop the rod by the front porch so I wouldn't forget it. After all the fruitless casts, I was always surprised when I felt the bite of a chum. But then all hell would break loose. They made strong porpoising runs and zig-zagged and thrashed. I think it takes longer to tire out a bright chum than any other salmon except springers. My arms would often be shaky and limp by the time I finally had the fish under enough control to slip up into the muddy shallows and tail it.

I always let them go, and then I'd give up chum fishing until the next year. I would snip the fly off, and impale it on the madrona with the other rusting flies from previous Decembers. That's the way I like to fly-fish for chum.

Public Beaches and Boat Launches

Abbreviations

Sea-run cutthroat: SRC
Red-tailed surfperch: RT
Marine bottomfish: MB
Coho: C
Chum: CM
Chinook: K
Flatfish: FF

Pacific Ocean

Makah Reservation: The Makah Indian Reservation extends from east of Neah Bay around Cape Flattery and down the coast to Makah Bay and beyond. You need a Recreational Use Permit to have access to the reservation, but it is free when you buy a tribal sportfishing license (available from the tribal office and Washburn's Store). Most fishing is on the Sooes and Waatch rivers (Map D5), for steelhead, salmon and trout, but the permit also lets you fish saltwater beaches. Regulations are subject to change, so it is always a good idea to call the tribal office (360-645-2201) for up-to-date information.

Olympic National Park Coastal Strip

This 45-mile stretch of Pacific Coast protects some of the last wilderness seashore in the lower 48 states. Day hikers can fish access points, but you have to backpack to reach the overwhelming bulk of the coastal strip. Backpackers must ford creeks, negotiate slippery boulder fields, climb sand ladders and steep overland trails, and wait for low tides to round headlands. You need to know what you're doing and exercise caution. Fishing rocky beaches is especially dangerous and not a good idea, because you can get knocked down by a rogue wave and not be able to get up on kelp-covered rocks. The red-tailed surfperch of sandy beaches are usually a safer target (when waves are calm), and sea-run cutthroat can be found seasonally around creek mouths.

Cape Alava to Shi Shi Beach: Less than eight miles long, this is the most difficult stretch to hike. It contains headlands that can only be rounded at low tide, slippery boulder patches, and steep overland trails with rope belays. The Ozette River can't be forded during winter and spring, and only at low tide during summer and autumn. Access from the Cape Alava Trail (Map D6) on the south and Makah Indian Reservation on the north.

North Coastal Strip: Stretching 20 miles, from the Quillayute River to Cape Alava, the north coast is only accessible at Rialto Beach (at the end of the Mora Road at the mouth of the Quillayute River) and at Sand Point and Cape Alava (via Ozette Loop Trails). Surfperch are available at Rialto Beach and Sand Point.

South Coastal Strip: Extends 17 miles from Third Beach near La Push to the mouth of the Hoh River, at the end of the Oil City Road. It includes the mouths of the Goodman and Mosquito creeks. Goodman Creek can't be forded at the mouth, and you must cross Mosquito Creek on overland trail on all but the lowest tides.

Beach Four: Located off Highway 101 three miles north of Kalaloch, this is one of the better surfperch beaches.

Kalaloch: The sandy beach provides perch, and the rocks have greenling and rockfish potential at extreme low tides. Very popular ONP campground and Kalaloch Lodge. Gas and supplies.

South Beach: Sandy beach and rustic campground approximately two miles south of Kalaloch. RT.

Pacific Beach State Park: Located 15 miles north of Ocean Shores on SR 109, this 10-acre ocean-front park has 2,300 feet of sandy beach access. Camping and surfperch.

Griffith-Priday Ocean State Park: A 364-acre day-use park with 8,316 feet of salt water beach and 9,950 feet on Copalis River. Within Copalis Beach. RT, C, SRC.

Strait of Juan de Fuca

Big Salmon Resort: Big Salmon Resort (360-645-2374) is located on the water, near the ramp and docks at Neah Bay.

Snow Creek Resort: (360-648-2284) The Snow Creek Resort is located just east of Neah Bay, a short run from the bottomfish grounds around Sail and Seal rocks and the offshore coho rips. It has a rail launch, tent and RV sites, and cabins.

Shipwreck Point Natural Reserve Conservation Area (NRCA): This 7-mile-long DNR beach extends from approximately 7.5 miles west of Sekiu to Sail River. Some private inholdings. Turnouts along Highway 112 provide access (Map D2). Mostly rocky shoreline, small MB, some surfperch in sandy pockets, SRC potential.

Clallam Bay Spit County Park: Thirty-three-acre park within the community of Clallam Bay contains over one mile of sand/gravel beach and the mouth of the Clallam River (often blocked by sand) (Map D1). SRC in the lagoon, and coho and steelhead from the bay.

Pillar Point County Park: Seasonal campground but year-round access to the beach near the mouth of the Pysht River. Boat launch. Extensive sand and mud flats with eelgrass. SRC, C, K.

Murdoch Beach DNR Access: (Map A27) Approximately one mile west of the Lyre River, at the end of PA-S-2510, this beach provides access to 30,000 feet of shoreline. It is wide at low tide, but harder going at high water, especially the 6,000 feet east of the access point. Some private uplands on eastern portion. Lots of rocks and kelp and bluffs but potential for marine bottomfish and sea-runs as you near the mouth of the Lyre River.

Mouth of Lyre River: At the mouth of the Lyre River, the Lyre River Park (360-928-3436) has access to the Strait of Juan de Fuca and lower river. RV and tent sites.

Whiskey Creek Beach: (Map A26) The Whiskey Creek Beach Resort (360-928-3489) has access to more than a mile of rocky beach, camping, cabins and a boat launch. Two miles east of the Lyre River. SRC, MB, RT. Daily access fee available during summer for anglers who aren't camping.

Crescent Bay: (Map A27) Crescent Beach and RV Park (360-928-3344) has one-half mile of private sandy beach and Salt Creek estuary access. Non-campers may pay an access fee. RT. SRC.

Salt Creek Recreation Area: Clallam County park at Tongue Point and the Salt Creek estuary. Includes east shore of the Salt Creek estuary downstream of Camp Hayden Road bridge. Camping. SRC.

Fresh water Bay County Park: Popular boat ramp for salmon anglers, but also has 1,450 feet of beach. The bay is relatively protected. Good skiff and kayak water. MB.

Elwha River Mouth: (Map A21) The dike trail at the east end of Place Road provides access to the estuary and salt water beach to the west. Consult regulations, because both areas are often closed. Also, all fishing will be prohibited for several years after Elwha dam removal begins (by 2012). The beach west of the river is large coble and drops off sharply, so wading isn't safe. When the area is open and conditions are right, you can connect with salmon and steelhead. Surfers are common.

Port of Port Angeles ramp: Ramps off Marine Drive and Ediz Hook provide access to the Strait of Juan de Fuca.

Port Angeles Waterfront Trail: (Map A20) You rarely see anyone fishing, but this pedestrian and bike path offers beach access at several sites. The sandy beach east of the old Rayonier Mill site and the mouth of Lees Creek are most suitable for wade fishing. Access is available at the end of Ennis Street (Map A19). SRC. C.

Dungeness National Wildlife Refuge (360-457-8451): Five-mile-long Dungeness Spit is the longest natural sand spit in North America. You can fish the Strait of Juan de Fuca side from its base to the lighthouse but probably won't catch anything. The inside (south side) of the spit is closed to public access year-round except for the first one-half mile, which is open between May 15 and September 30. It's a half-mile hike from the parking lot to the spit. Access fee, and dogs and bikes are prohibited. SRC.

Cline Spit County Park: Two-acre park with 240 feet of beach access and boat ramp that provides access to Dungeness Harbor and Dungeness Bay. Consult posted Dungeness NWR regulations, because there are seasonal and area closures. The only boat access to the spit is at the New Dungeness Lighthouse by permit from the Dungeness NWR. SRC. C. FF.

Oyster House (Port of Port Angeles): (Map A12) Rough boat launch east of Cline Spit. No water on large minus tides. Limited wading access.

Port Williams County Park (also Marlyn Nelson park): Northeast of Sequim, between Graysmarsh Farm and Sequim Bay, the park runs 1,000 feet to north to the Graysmarsh property line. May also hike a mile south on Gibson Spit to mouth of Sequim Bay. Very rough boat launch (car-toppers). Lots of dog walkers. SRC. C.

John Wayne Marina: A full-service marina, with boat launch and moorage. Boat access to Sequim Bay and the eastern strait. (360-417-3440).

Sequim Bay State Park: Full-service state park on south Sequim Bay. Boat ramp, moorage (removed in winter) and 4,909 feet of beach. SRC. FF.

Panorama Vista County Beach Access (DNR Beach 411): Extends three miles on Miller Peninsula from the end of Travis Spit to the middle of Thompson Spit. Access from East Sequim Bay Road and Panoramo Vista Road (Map A11). Largely cobble and gravel except for the spits. Eastern portion may eventually be included in the planned Miller Peninsula State Park. SRC.

Gardiner Boat Ramp/Lagoon: Port of Port Townsend boat ramp off Gardiner Beach Road.

Admiralty Inlet

Fort Worden State Park: (Map A10) All of the beach within the park is accessible, but virtually all fishing occurs between the boat ramp (Map A9) and Point Wilson lighthouse. This is one of Puget Sound's most productive salmon beaches, and coho are taken during late summer and early autumn when the season is open. Camping. Boat ramp, with seasonal floats.

Old Fort Townsend State Park: This 367-acre park has 3,960 feet of beach on Port Townsend Bay (Map A8). Camping. SRC.C.

WDFW Chimacum Creek Mouth Access: (Map A6) Located on Port Townsend Bay in Irondale, this sandy/gravel beach extends from the creek south 3,000 feet to Irondale County Park. Day-use park. Access from parking area at end of Moore Road. Sea-runs year-round and coho during September and early October.

Lions Club Park: (Map A4) Jefferson County park on SR 116, at east end of bridge between the mainland and Indian Island. Access to Port Townsend Ship Canal–The Cut. SRC year-round.

South Indian Island County Park: (Map A4) More than a mile of beach on Oak Bay and the south end of

Government Cut. First right turn after Lions Club Park. Sea-run cutthroat and occasional coho in autumn.

Mystery Bay: Little fishing at this 10-acre marine park on Marrowstone Island near Nordland, but ramp provides good access for small boats to protected water between Indian and Marrowstone islands.

Fort Flagler State Park: Encompassing the entire north end of Marrowstone Island, 784-acre Fort Flagler has more than 19,000 feet of beach. It also offers camping, two launches (Map A2, A3), and a moorage dock (out 9/15-3/25). Best known for late-summer/fall coho fishing at Marrowstone Point (Map A1). Some SRC and flounder taken along north and west shore.

Oak Bay West County Park: On the west shore of Oak Bay, off Oak Bay Road. Provides access north and south of lagoon mouth. Camping.

Port of Port Townsend ramp: Located within the Port Townsend Boat Haven, this ramp makes for an easy run to Admiralty Inlet and Port Townsend.

Lower Hadlock ramp: This ramp provides access to Port Townsend Bay and the mouth of Chimacum Creek. It is often covered by sand in winter.

Hood Canal

Matts Matts: Port of Port Townsend boat launch north of Port Ludlow.

Port Ludlow Marina: Private marina at Resort at Port Ludlow, with moorage, gas, supplies and a hoist ramp.

Shine Tidelands State Park: This long, narrow park at the northwest end of the Hood Canal Bridge provides nearly a mile of beach access. SRC. C.

Wolfe Property State Park: Just north of Shine Tidelands, at the end of Seven Sisters Road, this park continues beach access north to the spit that encloses Bywater Bay. SRC. C.

Hicks County Park: (Map B1) Rough launch for car-toppers on Shine Road south of the Hood Canal Bridge. Don't try it on tides lower than +5 feet. SRC.

WDFW Quilcene Bay Tidelands: (Map B2) Primarily a shellfish beach, it provides anglers with kayaks, skiffs and canoes high-tide access to upper Quilcene Bay. Get out before you are stranded by receding tide. On Linger Longer Road south of Quilcene. SRC. C. CM.

Quilcene Marina: At the end of Linger Longer Road, this Port of Port Townsend facility has a concrete launch, moorage, and gasoline. Adjacent swimming beach provides limited access when hatchery silvers move through Quilcene Bay in September. MB.

Point Whitney Ramp: A rough WDFW launch at the end of Bee Mill Road north of Brinnon. Short run to Quilcene and Dabob bays. Some cutthroat and coho fishing from one-half mile of beach access west and south of the ramp. Ramp is covered by sand in winter.

Dosewallips State Park: Straddling the mouth of the Dosewallips River within the hamlet of Brinnon, this is one of the most popular state parks. It has 5,500 feet of salt water beach. Also more than 5,000 feet of river access, but the lower Dosewallips is closed much of the year. Camping. SRC. C. CM.

WDFW Duckabush Tidelands: (Map B3) This large tideflat and saltmarsh at the mouth of the Duckabush River provides access to tidal pools, sloughs and Hood Canal beach. Parking on WDFW property on the southwest side of Highway 101 is much safer than on the road. SRC. C. CM.

Triton Cove State Park: Year-round launch provides access to central canal estuaries and creek mouths. Steep and exposed to north winds during summer blows. No camping or beach access.

Mike's Beach Resort: Scuba diving is the main show but the launch (fee) provides access to central Hood Canal.

Eagle Creek Tidelands: (Map B5) Located three miles north of Lilliwaup, this beach provides wading access for cutthroat, coho and chum.

Lilliwaup State Park: (Map B6) No campground or hiking, but this state park does offer more than a mile of public beach. Parking and access via steep stairs on the north side of Lilliwaup Bay. SRC. C. CM.

Hood Canal Recreational Park (Tacoma PUD): Closest ramp to Potlatch State Park and the mouth of the Skokomish River. Day use. SRC. C. CM. K.

Potlatch State Park: This 57-acre park is located between Shelton and Hoodsport. It has 9,500 feet of beach access and small mooring buoys (fee). Camping. SRC. C. CM. K.

Hood Canal Marina: In Union on the canal's Great Bend, this marina offers a launch and moorage. Access to Annas Bay and Skokomish River delta. SRC. C. CM. K.

Section 6
The Backcountry

Fly tied by Doug Rose.

Johnston's Olympic Alevin

Hook: Limerick 6X, 10 or 12
Body: Tinsel, silver oval
Yolk Sac: Yarn clipped to shape, red or orange
Wing: Polar bear substitute, white
Overwing: Badger hackle, beige

Many years ago, a friend gave me a trout survey of the mountain lakes in Olympic National Forest. It was written by James Johnston, a WDFW fish biologist who became something of a legend among high-lake trout anglers. A short essay at the end of the report, "Fly-fishing the High Olympic Lakes," *distinguished Johnston's report from other scientific papers. In it, he recommended six patterns for Olympic high-country lakes: a Carey Special, as a dragonfly nymph; a shrimp pattern; a midge pupa; a caddis dry fly; an ant pattern for autumn and, most interestingly, an alevin fly. It was designed to imitate juvenile trout right after hatching, when part of the yolk sac remains attached to the fish. Johnston fished it near shore and off creek mouths in June, July and August. Quite a few backcountry lakes in the Olympics have self-sustaining populations of trout, especially brook trout, and brookies and cutthroat routinely prey upon small fish. Give this pattern a try.*

Chapter Nineteen

Winter Camp

The backcountry of Olympic National Park contains all of the attractions that other western national parks offer visitors—magnificent mountain vistas, subalpine meadows, ancient forests, and, for the fly-fisher, trout in rivers and mountain lakes. But the trout in some of the park's wilderness rivers are steelhead. Summer and winter steelhead spawn in the Sol Duc, North Fork Sol Duc, South Fork of the Calawah, Bogachiel, Hoh and South Fork of the Hoh, Queets, and both forks of the Quinault. They also returned to the upper North Fork of the Skokomish and Elwha before dams blocked their migratory paths, and will once again return to the Elwha backcountry when the Elwha dams come down.

The wild summer steelhead of West End rivers swim to the most distant, most remote spawning grounds. Probably none of the summer-run populations were historically large, and the Elwha may have supported the most due to the nature of its canyons and long mainstem. But anglers have been aware of the summer fish for a long time. In recent decades, the lovely 4- to 10-pounders native to the Calawah and Sol Duc have become rare, and the rain forest rivers' wild stocks have also declined markedly. "In some index areas on the South Fork of the Hoh we are only seeing wild fish numbers in the 10s and 20s," said Sam Brenkman, ONP fisheries biologists.

I can't emphasize enough that there aren't many summer fish in the backcountry these days and they probably aren't worth your time. But if you have a line in the water, weird things happen. I once met a guy from Manhattan who came out here to visit friends. He set aside one day for fishing, and followed a rain forest river up into the park, beyond the reach of the road. He had a 6-weight and was fishing a big bushy Royal Wulff. He hooked a summer steelhead early in the day. This is a guy used to catching 10-inch hatchery rainbows, and suddenly he's holding on to a 10-pound steelhead doing somersaults and peeling line. It shocked the hell out of him, but he managed to land it. He returned the next three years and fished the same area hard and didn't catch anything but smolts and small bull trout.

Steelhead water beyond the reach of the road.

The Queets is my favorite summer-run river, and solitude is its major attraction. There is no way to reach the drifts and runs above the Queets Campground without hiking, and you can't reach the trail unless you are willing to ford the river. The Queets Trail begins across the river from the campground, just a little upstream of Sams River. During low water, it isn't a terrible ford, but you need strong legs and a pair of wading staffs. This is what outdoor recreation planners call a social filter. It keeps casual anglers on the south side of the river with their cars and trucks and drift boats.

When I first began hiking into the upper Queets, I caught summer-runs on standard wet flies, patterns like Green Butt Skunks and Fall Favorites. Later, after I became enthralled with Haig-Brown and Bill McMillan, I began fishing flies on top. I skated Steelhead Bees, waked Steelhead Caddis, and fished the Lady Caroline on the greased line. It didn't really seem to matter. If you could find the fish, you could usually get them to bite. They were the classic wild coastal steelhead—four to about eight pounds or so, with an occasional 10-pounder. They liked to hang off tributary mouths, and in pools with overhanging trees for shade, and in the seams where two currents came together.

The winter steelhead stocks that return to the backcountry are in better shape than summer fish, but there are fewer opportunities to fish for them. The park waters of the Sol Duc, South Fork Calawah and the forks of the Quinault are closed during winter, and the Queets is too high to ford. That leaves the Hoh, South Fork of the Hoh, and Bogachiel. They are open during winter and have trails that roughly parallel them. The wilderness portions of these rivers are now all managed under catch-and-release regulations, with single barbless hooks and no bait permitted. Fewer fish are available in the backcountry than in the lower ends of the river, but there are also far fewer anglers.

There are more than 800 miles of trail in the Olympic backcountry.

The Bogachiel Trail (Map D20) provides the most extensive access of any of the winter fishing trails, although it isn't always in the best shape during winter. You must frequently skirt immense tangles of blow-down and knee-deep mud. If you hike far enough, you will encounter creeks that aren't safe to ford at high water. The trail begins in the national forest, off Undi Road, and enters the park at Mile 2.0. It continues for more than 32 miles to the flanks of Bogachiel Peak. During the winter and spring steelhead season, not that many anglers hike the trail, and those who do seldom venture past Flapjack Camp, 10 miles from the trailhead.

The season remains open through April 15 on the Bogachiel in the park, but park biologist Brenkman would just as soon you fished earlier in the winter. "I'm a little uneasy about having the season open to April 15 on the upper river," he said. "Most of the steelhead are spawning by then."

I have hiked and caught winter steelhead in the Bogachiel backcountry for a long time, but I didn't understand what a treasure it is until a few years ago. Looking at a map of the park on a rainy winter night, I noticed how much farther west the wilderness extends on the Bogachiel than other West End rivers. Its trailhead is on a roughly north/south line with the junction of Highway 101 and Upper Hoh Valley Road. That is more than 10 miles west of the park boundary on the Hoh, and you are directly north of the end of Upper Hoh Valley Road. The park boundary extends farther west on the Queets than the Bogachiel, but a raven flying straight north from the Queets Campground will intersect the Bogachiel more than 10 miles into the backcountry.

Think about that for a minute. The boundaries of the park and the configuration of roads in the western Olympics have kept a significant portion of the lower-elevation reaches of the Bogachiel in wilderness. This is very rare in the lower 48 states. There are many mountain river trails where you can fish for trout, and there are also many miles of wilderness river that you can float in drift boats and rafts. But low-elevation winter steelhead water that is inaccessible by road and with no upstream boat ramps, well, there just aren't many places like that left anymore. And low-gradient reaches of winter steelhead rivers have more holding water are much easier to fish with a wet-fly swing than steeper sections.

I have a fantasy about fishing the upper Bogachiel during winter from a camp like the ones elk outfitters provide in the Rockies and Blue mountains. It would have a packer's tent, the kind you can stand up in, with a wood stove and stovepipe through the roof. I would sleep on a cot, and there would be tarps that I cooked and ate under. I imagine we would have pancakes and fried eggs and ham after fishing in the morning, and supper would be stews and roasts that had simmered for hours in Dutch ovens. I know exactly the place where I would want the camp—a grassy glade surrounded by cottonwoods and big leaf maple on a terrace above the river.

That's the fantasy. The reality is that it's been incomprehensibly wet every time I've camped in the Bogachiel backcountry during winter. There are also a lot more hours of darkness than daylight during December and January, and I've spent most of my time in my tent. I have occasionally caught fish, but if you don't have a good book and plenty of candles for your lantern you'll go nuts. I eat granola, oranges, Ramen noodles, cheese, bagels and Vienna sausages. I cook the noodles over a camp stove that I am sort of afraid of, and my tent begins to ooze water at some point, even though it's seam-sealed.

I have always had a good time, but I've also always been glad when it was over and I was on my way back to Forks for biscuits and gravy and decent coffee.

Chapter Twenty

Mildred Lakes

The author fishing Mildred Lakes.

The high-elevation lakes of the Olympic Mountains aren't evenly distributed throughout the backcounty. When the uplift that created the Olympic Peninsula occurred, the sedimentary rocks were largely deposited in the central, western and southern portions of the mountains, while the harder basalts ended up in a scythe-shaped band on the north and east. Known today as the Crescent; Formation, this 60-mile-long swatch of tough igneous rock contains the largest concentration of mountain lakes in the Olympics. It extends east from Lake Crescent through Grand Valley and the upper Dungeness down Hood Canal to the ring of peaks above the North Fork of the Skokomish. Although probably all of these lakes were originally barren of trout, they were planted as early as the 1920s.

Not all of Crescenti Formation lakes contain fish today. Olympic National Park quit stocking mountain lakes in the 1970s. Many park lakes still have good populations of self-sustaining trout, mostly brookies and a few rainbow, but some lakes that contained trout are now fishless. Olympic National Forest is the principle landowner on the northeast and eastern flanks of the mountains, and virtually all of its high-elevation holdings are within federally recognized wilderness—the Buckhorn Wilderness on the north, the Brothers Wilderness in the middle, and the Mount Skokomish Wilderness on the south. These lakes are managed and monitored by the Forest Service, but the WDFW stocks a number of them on a regular basis.

I have hiked to most of the Crescenti Formation lakes at one time or another, but some of my favorites are the Mildred Lakes, three subalpine lakes at the head of the Hamma Hamma River. The scenery is stunning, with the ragged, snow-caps of the Sawtooth Range and Mount Lincoln framing the lakes to the west. They are within a short distance of each other, which is an important consideration in the high country, because trout can be red hot in one lake and lock-jawed in a nearby one. I also like the fact that, although the hike up to them is steep and something of a scramble, it is only about five miles. You can hike up one day, fish the evening and the following morning, and take your time hiking out during the afternoon.

Of course, the main reason I like the lakes is their fish. I talked to a fly-fisherman from Shelton the last time I was up there, and he told me that he has taken several 20-inch fish from the lakes over the years. That isn't just angler bull. During a survey in the 1970s, the WDFW seined fish to 17 inches in Big Lake, to 13 in Little Lake and 24 inches in Crescent Lake. I have never caught one over 14 inches, but they have all been fat, firm and vigorous. The lakes have the standard complement of subaquatic insects, but scuds are present in each lake and are certainly the reason the fish grow so large. If you keep a fish for the pan, you will often notice the deep-red flesh of trout that feed upon these meaty crustaceans.

The largest of the Mildred Lakes, the one furthest to the west, is known as Big Lake. It is approximately 38 acres, one of the Olympic's larger subalpine lakes. Rainbow and cutthroat appear to spawn naturally, but cutthroat have been stocked recently. The first lake you encounter when you reach the top of the trail is the smallest, only about six acres, and is called Little Lake. It also contains rainbow and cutthroat, and they show evidence of spawning as well. The final lake, the one in the rocky basin north of the trail, is called Crescent Lake. It has no natural reproduction, but regularly turns out the largest fish. Although it was planted with rainbows in the 1980s, cutthroat have been stocked recently.

For anyone over 50, getting up to Mildred Lakes is harder than catching its fish. From the trailhead (1,678 feet), the first lake is only 4.9 miles away and the elevation gain is only 3,850 feet, not a particularly steep pitch. But don't be deceived. There are some grueling patches on the way up. You don't need climbing gear and there isn't anything life threatening, but there are a couple of gullies that you must deal with and a tough rocky scramble just below the first lake. Getting up to Mildred Lakes isn't anywhere near as bad as Lake Constance or even Goat Lake, but you want good knees, good lungs and a sense of balance.

If you can handle that, I bet you'll have a great time. I always have.

Chapter Twenty-One

Elwha Backcountry Rainbows

The Elwha River wilderness.

If you want to catch resident rainbow trout on flies on a backpacking trip on the Olympic Peninsula, fish the Elwha River above Goblin's Gate. It's that simple. You will catch a few rainbows in other rivers, particularly the upper Graywolf and Dungeness, and the Sol Duc in the park. But the Elwha has more of them and larger ones and there is more river to fish and to hike. From the trailhead at Whiskey Bend to the point the Elwha River Trail forks away from the river and climbs to Low Divide, the pass between the Elwha and Quinault basins, there are more than 25 river miles. With the exception of several deep canyons, all of it is accessible to fly-fishers, and all of its trout are wild.

The entire Elwha will be closed to fishing for five years after the dams on the middle and lower river are removed, and biologists expect the resident rainbow population to decline as they compete with juvenile steelhead and salmon. But the Elwha was noted for co-existing rainbow and steelhead populations, and I suspect resident trout will continue

Photo Courtesy of Washington State Historical Society

Elinor Chittenden with summer steelhead from Elwah Backcountry, 1907.

to provide a fine fishery in the upper river. The average upper Elwha rainbow is around 10 inches, although 12- to 14-inch fish are common. I hear of 18-plus-inch trout, but I've never seen one. Genetic profiles of the Elwha's backcountry rainbows suggest close ties to the winter steelhead of West End rivers. Perhaps that is why they are such tail-walking, spray-kicking, high-jumping aerialists.

One of the nicest things about the Elwha backcountry is you can craft a trip that will fit anyone's hiking ability. The trailhead at Whiskey Bend (Map A25) is located high above and out of sight of the river, and the trail remains that way for more than nine miles as it skirts Rica Canyon and the Grand Canyon of the Elwha. But three short, steep spur trails a short distance from the trailhead provide access to the three miles of river between the canyons. This section of the Elwha is called Geyser Valley and it's where Captain Christie took his fine mess of trout in March of 1890. You can fish Geyser Valley as a day hike or an easy backpacking destination. It is far enough from the trailhead to feel like you've gotten away, but close enough to stash canned food, liquor and bulky sweaters in your pack.

The first fishing opportunity beyond Geyser Valley is at Mary Falls, approximately 8.8 miles from Whiskey Bend, but Elkhorn Ranger Station, 11.5 miles, makes a better base camp. From here, you can fish back toward Canyon Camp and upstream to Lost River (12.5 miles) and Remanns Cabin. The Goldie River flows into the Elwha a couple of miles upstream of Remanns Cabin. The reach between the Goldie and Hayes River, roughly four miles above Elkhorn, is known as Press Valley. It was named by the Christie party for the Seattle newspaper owners who financed their trip. Access to the river in Press Valley is excellent, and campsites are available at Tipperary or Chateau camps, a few miles downstream of the Hayes River ranger station.

The nine miles of trail between Hayes River and Chicago Camp (25.8 miles) are the wildest, most remote reaches of the Elwha. Veteran Olympic backcountry fly-fishers consider the section between Buckinghorse Creek and Chicago Camp the Elwha's "Holy Water." Chicago Camp is where Herb Crisler caught a dozen trout with a discarded leader and fly after wandering without food for days in the high country. It is also near the site of the Elinor Chittenden steelhead photo. That's right. Steelhead swam this far before the dams. The river doglegs to the northwest beyond Chicago Camp, and the Low Divide Trail veers south to Low Divide, at 3663 feet, the lowest pass in the Olympics.

Any time after mid-July is usually safe on the upper Elwha, as far as river level and water temperature go. Snorkel surveys have found that the trout are usually widely distributed during early and midsummer, but become scarce in September. I imagine they drop down to the canyons and inaccessible pools, where shade and deeper water keep the temperature down. Having said that, the Elwha backcountry is a sweet place in autumn. The elk are bugling. The cottonwoods are gold and the sky is electric blue. The river is low and cold and bright. The nights are cool, but you can have fires all the way to Chicago Camp. You can always find some deep water with hungry trout if you work at it.

You will see mayflies, especially *Baetis*, but the upper Elwha has always been considered caddis and stonefly water. October caddis are common in the lower reaches of the backcountry, especially Geyser Valley. So are salmonflies and golden stoneflies, and you can take trout on big hair wings during midsummer golden stone egg-laying flights. I am intrigued by a recent report that identified *Arctopsyche* caddis in the upper river. Also known as the great gray sedge, these caddis are large (imitated by size-6 larvae and adults), are common in the drift as juveniles, and emerge near dark. Terrestrial insects are probably as important as subaquatic ones during September and October.

Actually, I think you're missing the point if you are spending a lot of time dithering about bugs on the upper Elwha. I asked J.D. Love once what patterns he liked for resident trout and he said, "Oh, I usually just fish a Royal Wulff." I think J.D. had resident cutthroat in mind, but you won't go too far wrong on the Elwha with any of the Wulff patterns, and a small Grizzly Wulff is a fine yellow Sally pattern. I also like dropper rigs, anchored with a large black stonefly nymph or Bob's Possum Stone. The fastest action of the day on the Elwha often happens right before dark, and there is probably no better twilight fly than a large Parachute Adams. I also like soft hackles in the evening because I fish them downstream and can feel strikes that I would never see.

My favorite Elwha tale is about two college kids who fished it about 20 years ago. They were from somewhere back East, and had hitch-hiked West to fish and hike in national parks. The way I heard it, they hadn't even intended to visit the Olympics, but ended up in Seattle, saw the mountains, and hopped a ferry. Someone told them about the trout fishing in the Elwha backcountry and they decided to give it a shot. That, as they say, was that. They spent the rest of their vacation between Hayes River and Chicago Camp. Every week or so, they would stash their gear and hike out and buy more food and tippet and flies. Then they'd race back up the trail.

They would be in their mid-forties now. I bet they think of that summer a lot, and I bet when they do their blood pressure drops about 10 points.

Backcountry River Trails

With the exception of the Elwha, the headwater reaches of most Olympic Peninsula rivers do not support large resident trout populations. However, you can enjoy catch-and-release fishing for small rainbow, cutthroat and, occasionally, brook trout from some riverside trails. You may catch native char incidentally, but they are all protected under the ESA and must be released immediately. Summer and winter steelhead are available in the backcountry of some coastal rivers, but their numbers are small and trails only provide intermittent access.

Elwha River: (Map A25) Trailhead at Whiskey Bend. See Elwha Backcountry Rainbow chapter

Cameron Creek: Crosses Cameron Creek, which is partially glacial, a number of times in the first five miles

Upper Graywolf (from Three Forks): 5.4 miles to Cedar Creek Trail

Upper Dungeness: (Map A18) Trailhead on FR 2825; 3.4 miles to Camp Handy

Duckabush: Off and on river access from trailhead to Five Mile Camp, but also gorges and canyons; Ten Mile Camp only 1,500 feet elevation.

North Fork Skokomish: Parallels river for 5.3 miles to Big Log Camp, then intermittent access to Nine Stream

East Fork Quinault: Good access from Graves Creek to a couple of miles above O'Neil Camp (9 miles)

North Fork Quinault: Fishable off and on from North Fork Ranger Station to Rustler Creek; many canyons above.

Queets: Trailhead to Harlow Bottom best access

Hoh: From Ranger Station to Happy Four Shelter, 5.6 miles

Bogachiel: Relatively flat trail with off and on river access to Hyak Shelter, 17.4 miles

North Fork Sol Duc: Trail crosses river approximately one mile from Sol Duc Hot Springs Road, then again as it climbs to east

Backcountry Lakes

Abbreviations: Trout Sizes

Small: 1 to 7 inches
Medium: 8 to 11 inches
Large: 12 plus inches
Acres: a
Rainbow: RB
Eastern Brook: EB
Cutthroat: CT

Rain Forest

Sol Duc

Seven Lakes Basin (5 to 31a; 3,850-4,600 ft.): Discovered by Chris Morganroth in 1892, this 1,600-acre subalpine basin is 8.1 miles from the Canyon Creek trailhead at Sol Duc falls. You climb to 4,900 feet and gain 2,900 feet before dropping into the basin. Sol Duc Lake (31a) has a modest population of small EB and scuds. Long Lake (15a): Large population medium EB. Morganroth (10a): Some large EB and RB. Round (8a): Small population EB, but some are large, scuds. Lunch (8a): Large population EB with evidence of stunting, scuds. Lake #8 (7): RB and EB. No Name (8): Some large EB and RB and scuds. Y Lake (5): Small numbers medium to large EB.

Deer Lake (8a; 3,525 ft.): Near the end of Canyon Creek Trail, 2.9 miles from Sol Duc Falls. Elevation gain 1,525 feet. EB to 12 inches, in good condition due to scuds.

Mink Lake (10; 3,080 ft.): A pleasant late-spring or fall destination; 2.5 miles above the Sol Duc Hot Springs Resort. Elevation gain 1,404 feet. Mostly medium EB.

Hoh Basin

Hoh Lake (18a; 4,500 ft.): The Hoh River Trail is the first leg (9.5 mi.) of the nearly 15 miles to the lake, but switchbacks on the Hoh Lake Trail account for almost all of the 3,922-foot elevation gain. EB.

Elk Lake (13a.; 2,550 ft.): The Hoh River Trail provides the 14-mile route to this beautiful lake near the base of Mount Olympus. Less than 2,000-foot elevation gain. EB.

Quinault Basin

Irely Lake (4-20a; 550 ft.): The size of the lake depends on run-off. About a mile from the Big Creek Trailhead, this is the only interior lake in ONP that contains native cutthroat, rainbow (possibly steelhead smolts) and char. Some large CT. Catch-and-release and artificial lures and flies with single barbless hooks.

Sundown Lake (3a; 3,900 ft.): Located 7.4 miles from the Graves Creek Ranger Station on the Graves Creek Trail. Elevation gain 2,254 feet. RB and EB.

Rain Shadow

Lake Crescent Basin

Eagle Lakes (<1a; 2,625-3,075 ft.): On Aurora Ridge, above Lake Crescent's south shore. EB in largest lake in last ONP survey.

Happy Lake (6a; 4,875 ft.): Approximately 5.5 miles from the Happy Lake Ridge Trailhead on the Olympic Hot Springs Road. EB.

Elwha Basin

Boulder Lake (8a; 4,340 ft.): Steady 2.8-mile climb from old Olympic Hot Springs Campground (hike-in); in circque valley beneath Appleton Pass. EB.

Margaret and Mary (6 and 3 a; 3,550 ft.): At Low Divide, the pass between the Elwha and Quinault watersheds. Mary had EB in the last ONP high-lakes survey, but none were found in Margaret.

Martins Lakes: Southeast of Low Divide. No fish.

Lake Creek Basin

Angeles Lake (19a; 4,196 ft.): A stunning cirque lake at the base of Mount Angeles. The Lake Angeles Trail (also called Klahanne Ridge Trail) begins near Heart of the Hills Campground. It gains 2,356 feet on the 3.4-mile climb to the lake. Difficult bank access for fly-fishers. EB.

Morse Creek Basin

P.J. Lake (2a; 4,700 ft.): Trailhead on Obstruction Point Road is snowbound long after April opener. Steep .9-mile drop to lake. Large population of small EB.

Dungeness/Graywolf Basin

Grand Valley Lakes {Grand (13a; 4,700), Moose (9a; 5,100), Gladys (6a; 5,400)}: The trailhead at the end of Obstruction Point Road (6,150 ft.) is usually not accessible until late June. The Grand Pass Trail descends 3.7 miles to Grand Valley. Grand Lake; Very large population of EB, most under 10, a few small RB; scuds and snails. Moose: Small EB, most feed on chironmids and terrestrials. Gladys: Modest population medium EB, feed largely on Chironomids and ants during summer. Don't push the season at either end, because hikers have died trying to hike out during blizzards.

Cedar Lake (21a; 5,275ft.): One of the most lightly-visited backcountry lakes. Since the lower Graywolf Bridge washed out, the most direct route is 4.3 miles down the Three Forks Trail from Blue Mountain, then 7.5 miles up the Graywolf Trail and Cedar Lake Way Trail. The return trip involves a 3,300-foot climb from Three Forks back up to the trailhead in a little more than 4 miles. You may want to wait until the Graywolf Bridge is repaired, which will let you hike up the Lower Graywolf Trail for 10 miles to Three Forks. RB.

Royal Lake (2a; 5,100 ft.): The elevation gain from the Upper Dungeness Trailhead to Royal Basin is only 2,630 feet over 7.1 miles, more than worth the effort to see one of the Olympics' most spectacular mountain basins. Medium-sized EB.

Goat Lake (8a; 5,930 ft.): There isn't even an official trail into it, but the fragile subalpine habitat around Goat Lake has been damaged from heavy angler traffic, and the Forest Service has recommended the state stop stocking the lake. It received Atlantic salmon plants during the 1980s, and the current 8.9-pound state record was taken from the lake. There is no natural reproduction, and rainbows replaced salmon in the 1990s. The Upper Dungeness Trail provides access to Camp Handy (3.2 mi.), and then you ford the river and find the way trail. It climbs 1.8 miles to the lake, with a grueling 2,830-foot elevation gain, the last part on loose scree. Large RB. Scuds and small leeches.

Silver Lakes (1 and 2a; 5,450 ft.): The Mount Townsend and Silver Lakes trails climb a modest 2,150 feet over 5.5 miles to the lakes. Small EB in upper lake. Often crowded.

Hood Canal

Buckhorn Lake (<1a; 5,150 ft.): Located north of Iron Mountain, Buckhorn Lake contains a self-sustaining population of small EB. It is 6.1 miles (2,000-foot elevation gain) up the Tubal Cain Trail and Buckhorn Lake Way Trail.

Big Quilcene Basin

Charlia Lakes (3 and 9a; 5,500-5,700 ft.): Whether you approach them from the Big Quilcene side (7.3 miles on the Upper Big Quilcene Trail and Charlia Lake Way Trail) or from the Dungeness (7.7 mile on Upper Dungeness Trail and Charlia Lake Way trail) it requires time and stamina. You even have to heel 1,000 feet down to the lakes at the end of the way trail. Stocked since the 1940s with everything from EB to RB to Atlantic salmon. Only the lower lake has fish. Medium EB and CT may spawn naturally.

Home Lake (1.5a; 5,300 ft.): The shortest distance to Home Lake is up the Dosewallips Trail to the Constance Pass Trail, but the southern side of Constance Pass Trail is brutally steep. It's longer but easier on the Upper Big Quilcene Trail to Marmot Pass and the northern portion of Constance Pass Trail. EB.

Harrison Lake (<1a; 4,750 ft.): Located 3.7 miles from Tunnel Creek Trail trailhead, Harrison Lake has self-sustaining small EB. Similarly-sized Karnes Lake is just north of Harrision but hasn't had trout in recent surveys. Elevation gain 2,150 ft.

Dosewallips Basin

Lake Constance (11a; 4,900 ft.): Don't even consider this unless you have good balance, aren't timid, and are in really good shape, because the short 2.1-mile scramble to Lake Constance is widely-acknowledgedas the most brutal in the Olympics. Elevation gain is 3,250 feet. Small EB with evidence of stunting. The washout on the Dosewallips Road now requires a 3.5-mile hike to the trailhead.

Jupiter Lakes (<1 to 6a; 3,500-4,800 ft.): This complex of lakes straddles Mount Jupiter's north flank. There is no official trail into the lakes but you can reach them by hiking approximately six miles up the Mount Jupiter Trail and then down the angler's way trail to the eastern lakes. Lake 4 is the closest to the trail and has red copepods, which produce fish to 15 inches. The next lake to the west, Lake 3, has difficult access due to cliffs. Continuing west, Lake 2 had some large RB but is now planted with WSC. Lake 1 has medium-sized rainbow but no natural reproduction. Lakes 5 and 6, which are apart from the other lakes to the west, contain EB and CT, with some large fish. You are completely on your own here and it's no place for novice hikers or people in poor physical condition.

Duckabush Basin

La Crosse, Buck, Hart (4,800-5,050 ft.): Located in the headwaters of the Duckabush River, between the snow fields on Mount LaCrosse and Mount Duckabush. You have to hike more than 20 miles up Duckabush Trail to reach them. Park surveys only found fish in Hart Lake.

Hamma Hamma Basin

Lower Lena Lake (55a; 1,800ft.): Lower Lena receives more public use than any other mountain lake in Olympic National Forest. Moderate 1,400-foot gain on three-mile hike from trailhead near Lena Creek Campground. Don't anticipate solitude during the summer, but the lake can be deserted on spring and autumn weekdays. Often very low late in autumn. Stocked since 1930s. Medium CT. RB. EB.

Upper Lena Lake (25a; 4,500 ft.): The 3.9-mile trail beyond Lower Lena to Upper Lena Lake (2,450-foot elevation gain) is steeper and rockier. Upper Lena is one of the few park lakes with rainbow but no brookies. They are small to medium-sized, and their pale flesh suggests a lack of scuds.

Scout (25 a; 4,250 ft.): Scout Lake drains to the Duckabush but is easier to consider with Hamma Hamma basin lakes because that is the way you approach it. A rocky three-mile way trail from Upper Lena provides access. Medium-sized population of RB to 13-plus-inches, with 9 average. No camping at lake.

Mildred Lakes (6-38 a; 3850-3900 ft.): Scuds in all three lakes account for their large, well-conditioned trout. "Big Lake" (the westernmost): 38 acres, deepest, has RB and CT. "Little Lake" (first lake on trail):10 acres, RB and CT. "Crescent Lake" (off main trail to the north): 6 acres, some large CT. Although only 4 1/2 miles, Mildred Lake Way Trail gains 2,170 feet, and has several gullies and rocky scrambles.

North Fork Skokomish Basin

Wagonwheel Lake (3a; 4,150 ft.): Located on Cooper Mountain two miles north of Lake Cushman, Wagonwheel Lake is a very steep 2.9-mile hike few anglers attempt. RB and scuds. Trailhead is on the Lake Cushman Road in the park. Gains a rugged 3,200 feet.

Flapjack Lakes (6 and 10a.; 3,900 ft.): These two lakes are located just across Sawtooth Ridge from Mildred Lakes, but are within ONP. The North Fork Skokomish Trail is a relatively flat 3.8 miles to the Flapjack Lakes Trail, which then climbs from 785 to 3,900 feet over four miles. Despite being two of the most popular high lakes in the park (camping reservations are required), both contain some large fish. Upper Lake: BT and RB average, respectively, 8 and 7 inches. Lower Lake: BT average 11 inches and RB 8. Fish prey heavily on scuds and are in very good condition.

Black and White Lakes (total 3a; 4,500 ft.): These lakes contained no fish in the last ONP high-lakes survey.

Smith Lake (11a; 4,000 ft.): Although it is only 2.2 miles from Flapjack Lakes, the Smith Lake Way Trail is steep, rocky and often hard to follow. EB.

Part III

An Orange Heron tied by the master and originator himself, Syd Glasso.

Chapter Twenty-Two

Glasso and Wentworth Speys

Fly originated and tied by Syd Glasso.

With its mallard flank wings, Glasso's Brown Heron is nearly identical to the original Scottish Spey flies.

The term Spey fly has taken on a certain elasticity in the decades since Syd Glasso first fished his Orange Heron and Sol Duc Spey on West End rivers. Just as the term rain forest is now used to describe just about any patch of woods in the Pacific Northwest that has large trees and ferns, Spey fly is now used to describe any pattern with feather wings that ride low over the hook and long, swept-back hackle. I even saw a "Spey" fly recently with a hair wing, for God's sakes. But the flies Glasso created are quite faithful to their namesakes, the Atlantic salmon flies of Scotland's Spey River, and they have unifying characteristics and materials.

Take a look at that great Scottish Grande Dame, the Lady Caroline, the only traditional Spey that most fly-fishers know on sight. According to legend, it was created by Gordon Shanks, the long-serving ghillie at Grant Castle, on the banks of the Spey. It is tied on a long-shanked hook and originally had a wool body and gold or silver tinsel ribs. The Lady Caroline doesn't have a tail, as some Speys did, but it usually had a tinsel tag. Its wings are bronze mallard flank, tied low over the body. The original hackle was Spey cock, an extinct local bird, and a turn or two of teal for a collar. The low angle of the wing and hackle create the elegant silhouette of a Spey fly.

Although Glasso's flies were unlike anything on the West Coast when he created them, they would have been instantly recognizable to Shanks. They have the same low profile and tented wings as the Scottish dressings. They also employ dubbing for the forward part of the body, although he favored silk floss on their aft ends. Until it was outlawed, Glasso used heron for body hackle, either palmered or tied forward of the second rib turn. As in the Scottish patterns, he used tinsel for flash and to secure the hackle stems and reinforce the bodies. Glasso's Brown Heron is nearly indistinguishable from the Scottish pattern of the same name. The principal difference between Glasso's flies and the Scottish originals is they used hotter colors and usually had hackle tip wings rather than mallard flank.

If Glasso's Speys weren't that different from the original Spey flies, they were a world apart from other West Coast steelhead flies of the 1950s and '60s—that is, south of British Columbia, where British ex-patriots Roderick Haig-Brown and General Noel Money had fished the Lady Caroline since the 1920s. Hair-winged steelhead flies had all but replaced feather wings south of the border by the 1940s. Most were tied on heavy, short-shanked hooks and either had chenille or tinsel bodies. Their wings were cocked up at a jaunty angle, and the hackles were short and all but hidden. With their sleek lines, long webby hackles and tented wings, their low-water hooks and tiny onyx teardrop heads, Glasso's Speys stood out from traditional West Coast steelhead flies like a Harlequin duck among a flock of coots.

For all their elegance, it is easy to forget that Glasso designed his flies to catch fish. He told Walter Johnson that he substituted hackle tip wings for the mallard flank because they had more action in the water. He used hot colors because he thought they would be more visible in the winter murk of the Sol Duc and Calawah. Indeed, Glasso said that one of the reasons he was initially drawn to Spey flies was because the Scottish rivers were often high and dirty during their fishing season, and he thought dressings that worked on those rivers might stand a chance on the peninsula's even higher and faster water. As much as he loved beautiful things—he drove Porsches and fished cane rods and Hardy reels—the first order of business with Glasso was catching steelhead.

The 21-pound Sol Duc steelhead that hit Dick Wentworth's Mr. Glasso Spey fly. (It is memorialized in Jack Datisman's painting in the Forks Thriftway.)

"It was nothing for him to catch 30 fish by the end of the season and the season ended in February a lot of the time back then," said Dick Wentworth, Glasso's most well-known protégé and a superb Spey fly tier in his own right. "He used to say 'A fly-fisherman isn't worth his salt if he doesn't have a winter run on a fly by Thanksgiving."

Glasso's Sol Duc won him top honors in the steelhead category of the 1958 *Field & Stream* fishing contest, taking an 18-pound 12-ounce fish. A few years later, Dick caught two fish on three casts with the Sol Duc, and in March of 1981, he landed a 21-pound steelhead on a Spey fly of his own design, the Mr. Glasso, that he named in honor of his mentor.

Legend has it that the Orange Heron was the first Spey fly that Glasso created, but Dick Wentworth has shown me its predecessor, the Gray and Orange. "See that," he said as we sat in the den of his Forks home, "That came first." The Gray and Orange features the same light gray and bright orange color scheme as the Orange Heron but is slightly more subdued and more buggy. "I think the Chappie might have influenced it a little." The Chappie is an old steelhead and sea-run cutthroat fly that Los Angeles area writer C.L. "Outdoor" Franklin fished for decades on the Klamath and Trinity rivers. Along with the Silver Hilton and Spruce fly, it was one of the few feather wings still in widespread use when Glasso began creating his Spey flies.

Glasso had precise ideas about where and when to fish his flies, and he shared them with Trey Combs in *Steelhead Fly-fishing and Flies*. He recommended the Polar Shrimp, not one of his own patterns, in sizes 1 and 1/0 for the Hoh and Queets, but he tied it Spey fashion, with long white hackle tip wings rather than bucktail. For winter fishing on the clearer running Quillayute System rivers, he selected his Sol Duc in size 1 and Sol Duc Spey in 1 and 1/0, both of which feature hot-orange and yellow. Glasso liked the Orange Heron (1/0), Sol Duc Dark (1) and Dick Wentworth's Quillayute (1, 1/0) for the Quillayute tributaries in springtime.

In the half century since he created the Northwest's first Spey flies, Glasso's dressings have become the most celebrated in steelheading and his influence has spread around the world. Glasso originals fetch as much as $1,500 at auction, and some of the most gifted fly tiers of the last generation, artists such as Dave McNeese and Steve Gobin, have devoted much of their efforts to Spey flies. John Shewey's *Spey Flies & Dee Flies* and Bob Veverka's *Spey Flies: How to Tie Them* are superb contributions to steelhead fly-fishing literature. While some of the original materials that the Scottish ghillies and Glasso employed are now unavailable, excellent substitutes such as schlappen and blue-winged pheasant and Angora goat are easy to obtain.

For all their acclaim, it always strikes me as a little sad that so few anglers actually fish Spey flies today, even on the Olympic Peninsula. Fly-fishers you encounter on the Sol Duc are much more likely to have a huge Bunny Leech or Marabou Spider on their keeper ring—if not an egg pattern beneath a damned float—than a Sol Duc Spey. They will tell you that Speys are too hard to tie or take too much time. My favorite excuse is they don't actually work very well for steelhead, that they don't track properly. Whenever I hear that, I think of my friend, Jack Datisman's painting, "Mr. Glasso."

It's on display in the Forks Thriftyway, and it shows a large winter steelhead about to take a fly. The fly in the painting is the Mr. Glasso created by Dick Wentworth, and the fish is a representation of the 21-pounder Dick took with it in March of 1983.

Fortunately, despite their lack of widespread use, the legacy of Glasso's flies remains vibrant on the Olympic Peninsula. Dick Wentworth still fishes his great friend's patterns and his own Spey dressings. Although their numbers are small, a new generation of tiers has embraced the high standards of Glasso's craftsmanship. If there is an emblematic signature linking Glasso with these tiers, it is a fondness for feather wings. You see lots of hair wings out here, but the most beautiful and effective local patterns have feather wings. The feathers in John Alevras' Hoh River Claret and James Garrett's Kate are green-winged teal. They are ostrich in Don Kaas's Feather Dusters. They are hackle tips in Dave Steinbaugh's Isabella and John McMillan's Optimist.

If there is an Olympic Peninsula steelhead fly-fishing heritate it is characterized by sleek, sparse flies with feather wings.

Orange Heron—Syd Glasso

Body: rear 2/3 orange silk; front 1/3 hot-orange seal or substitute
Rib: tinsel, medium flat and medium oval
Hackle: gray heron or substitute
Throat: teal or hooded merganser flank
Wing: four hot-orange hackle tips
Head: red

Brown Heron—Syd Glasso

Body: rear, orange silk; front hot-orange seal or substitute
Rib: flat silver, medium; oval silver, small
Hackle: gray heron or substitute
Throat: teal, widgeon or hooded merganser
Wing: bronze mallard or widgeon
Head: red
Wing: bronze mallard, widgeon or merganser

Gold Heron—Syd Glasso

Body: rear two thirds flat gold tinsel; front, orange seal dubbing
Rib: gold, oval
Hackle: gray heron
Throat: widgeon or merganser
Head: orange

Courtesan—Syd Glasso

Tied by Dick Wentworth.

Body: rear, orange floss; front, hot-orange seal or substitute
Rib: flat silver
Hackle: schlappen, long, soft brown fibers
Throat: widgeon, merganser or none
Wing: four orange hackle tips
Head: red

Sol Duc—Syd Glasso

Tied by Dick Wentworth.

Tip: tinsel, flat silver
Tail: golden pheasant crest
Body: rear, orange floss; front, hot-orange seal or substitute
Rib: tinsel, flat silver
Body hackle: schlappen, yellow, from second tinsel turn
Throat: teal, one turn
Wing: four hot-orange hackle tips
Topping: golden pheasant crest
Head: red thread

Sol Duc Spey—Syd Glasso

Tied by Dick Wentworth.

Tag: tinsel, flat silver
Body: rear, orange silk; front, hot-orange seal or dubbing
Rib: flat silver tinsel
Hackle: schlappen, yellow, from second tinsel turn
Throat: heron substitute, dyed black
Wing: four hot-orange hackle tips
Head: red

Sol Duc Dark

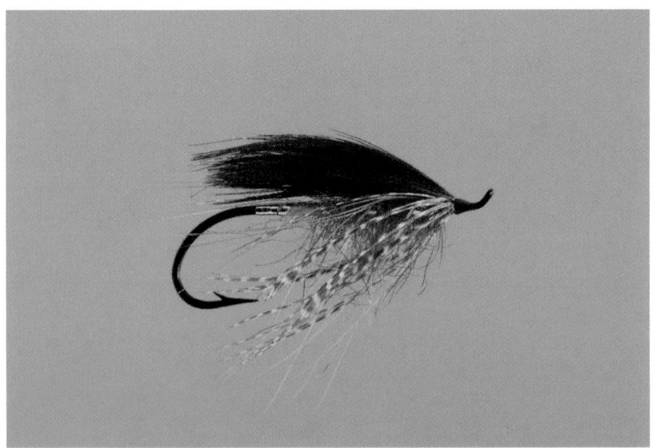

Tied by Dick Wentworth.

Tip: tinsel, oval narrow silver
Tail: Amherst pheasant crest
Body: rear, orange silk; front, hot-orange seal or dubbing
Ribs: tinsel, silver flat and silver fine oval
Hackle: schlappen, yellow, from second turn
Throat: teal flank, one turn
Wing: four matching golden pheasant body feathers, red
Topping: Lady Amherst pheasant crest
Head: red thread

Quillayute—Dick Wentworth

Tag: silver
Tail: Amherst topping
Body: rear, orange silk floss; front, hot-orange seal or substitute
Rib: tinsel, medium, flat
Hackle: teal flank, from second tinsel turn
Throat: heron substitute, dyed black
Wing: four matching golden pheasant flank feathers
Topping: Amherst pheasant

Mr. Glasso—Dick Wentworth

Body: rear, silk floss; front, hot-orange seal or substitute
Rib: tinsel, silver medium flat and silver oval
Hackle: blue-eared pheasant, dyed black
Throat: guinea, dyed hot-orange
Wing: four hot-orange hackle tips
Head: red

Chapter Twenty-Three

When Entomology Matters

Jo Marie Uhlman working a hair-wing on the Quinault during October caddis season.

I spent an early summer day a few years ago floating the middle Sol Duc with one of the Olympic Peninsula's best steelhead fly-fishers. He takes as many winter fish on flies in a year as most anglers do in their lives, and he is also an excellent summer steelhead and cutthroat fly-fisherman. We launched at Maxfield Road, and it was late afternoon by the time we pulled out at the Whitcomb-Dimmel Ramp.

"Look," I said. "Golden stones. Those are the first I've seen this year."

"Really. I always wondered what they were."

That is my favorite anecdote about the relative importance of aquatic entomology on the Olympic Peninsula. In most areas of the country, a working knowledge of sub-aquatic and terrestrial insects is a critical component of fly-fishing. The study of the insects that trout eat and the flies that imitate them is also the subject of the majority of fly-fishing literature. But nearly all the fish we catch on Olympic Peninsula rivers are anadromous—that is, they reside in fresh water as juveniles, attain the bulk of their size in salt water, then return to rivers to spawn. With the exception of cutthroat and the occasional summer steelhead, the adult fish do not feed on their spawning journeys.

Having said this, there are times and places where a basic understanding of the insects in Olympic Peninsula rivers is important. The Elwha and North Fork Skokomish above the dams are the obvious places to practice matching the hatch for resident trout. But sea-runs will selectively feed on blue-winged olives on frosty October mornings on the upper Sol Duc and South Fork of the Calawah. I've also seen Graywolf rainbows refuse everything except a Yellow Sally imitation, and Bogachiel River cutthroat demand a skittering hair-wing during an October caddis egg-laying flight.

". . . I will herewith set forth my idea as to the proper assortment for a day's fishing in the Olympic Mountain streams," E. B. Webster wrote in *Fishing in the Olympics* (1922): "First you should select: Six brown hackles; Then add three coachmen, three professors, and Six brown hackles."

You will probably want more flies than that, but you should be able to take most resident trout in the Olympics with patterns that imitate the following 10 insects.

Blue-winged Olives: These tiny mayflies have multiple broods annually, and the fall insects are smaller than those in spring. They seem most important in late fall, when other insect activity is reduced. Fish size 16-20 BWO emergers or *Baetis* Sparkle Duns on long, fine tippets. This is as demanding as trout fishing gets on the peninsula.

Pale Morning Duns: PMDs are early to mid-summer insects on most Olympic Peninsula rivers, although you encounter them later at higher elevations. A size 12-16 PMD Comparadun is a fine adult pattern, while a Pheasant Tail is a good nymph. Nymphs and adults are most abundant in soft water, and duns can appear any time of day.

Green Drakes: You won't see western green drakes very often, and you can't depend on them to hatch at a given time or place. They are large and Elwha rainbows target them in early summer. Size 10 and 12 Green Drake Cripples and Sparkle Duns (Blue Ribbon Flies) are fine adult patterns. Skate-Winged Olives, a slightly smaller *drunella*, hatch during autumn on the Elwha and Sol Duc.

Hydropshyche: Research has indicated that these spotted caddis flies are found in more than 60 percent of western Washington "coastal" rivers and Puget Sound streams. Fish size 8-14 Gold Ribbed Hare's Ears and LaFontaine's Emergent Sparkle Pupa for the larva and pupa, and Blue Ribbon Flies' Iris Caddis for the adult.

Rhyacophilla: The larval stage of these insects, the famous "Green Rock Worm," crawls over rocky bottoms in search of food. A size 10-14 Partridge and Green fished deeply will often take fish when there is no surface activity, and a Diving Caddis imitates females swimming to the bottom to deposit eggs. The X Caddis is a fine dry fly.

October Caddis: The bottoms of large and medium-size rivers are often littered with Dicosmoecus larvae during summer. Despite its name, a local fly, Bob's Possum Stone, in size 6 or 8 is a great larva pattern. Bill McMillan's Steelhead Caddis fished under tension is an excellent fly egg-laying females are over the water.

Salmonfly: The Sol Duc and Elwha seem to have the most salmonflies, but the adults hatch in late April, before the trout season is open on the upper rivers. However, the nymphs are available to trout year-round, and James Garrett's Black and Orange Olympic Stonefly will take large rainbows once the season opens in June.

Golden Stonefly: The peninsula has two closely related species that hatch in July and early August—the western stonefly and golden stonefly—but don't worry about the differences. Fish Curt's Woven Stone (size 6 & 8) as a nymph, and Bill McMillan's Steelhead Caddis (yellow body) on top in late afternoon and evening.

Yellow Sallies: These late-summer and autumn stoneflies are available on large rivers and mountain creeks. A size 12-16 Elk Hair Caddis will take resident cutthroat from the edges of plunge pools, and a Partridge and Yellow soft hackle fished on a downstream swing will take Elwha and Graywolf rainbows from gentle runs.

You don't want to forget about terrestrials, of course, because beetles, ants and grasshoppers are also important, especially during autumn. And cutthroat eat a lot of sculpins and crayfish so you should carry a couple Muddler Minnows. But you needn't take this very far. The Olympic Peninsula is anadromous fish country, not Yellowstone. If you are spending a lot of time thinking about insects, you are missing the point of this place. It's sort of like focusing on the floor tiles and woodwork in the Louvre.

Chapter Twenty-Four

Six Flies for Olympic Peninsula Lakes

Dick Wentworth fishing Yahoo Lake, in the upper Clearwater River basin.

At one time my wife and I lived a couple miles from Gibbs Lake. It is your classic coastal trout lake, surrounded by a fringe of Douglas fir, red cedar and a tangle of cattails and lily pads. In springtime, splashy pink rhododendron blossoms brighten the shoreline, and it has the obligatory osprey nest. It contains hatchery rainbow trout, and lately the State has been planting it with a few hundred "triploid" rainbow. Although you seldom catch them, Gibbs also has a few migratory cutthroat. It is open year-round, with selective fishery and catch-and-release regulations for trout, but is more or less deserted after October.

Eliana and I got into the habit of walking around the lake on Thanksgiving mornings. She would put the turkey in the oven, and we would drive over to the lake with Lily, our yellow Labrador. It was usually rainy, often with wind, but once it was a warm soft day, with low cloud cover. A huge midge hatch was underway. There were so many rises it looked like it was sprinkling. Many were splashy little affairs,

This nearly 15-inch mountain-lake brook trout had numerous scuds in its stomach.

the sign of small fish, but every once in a while you would see a slow-motion boil, followed by a sucking swirl. I had no problem believing they were large trout, because my friend George Binney's wife Jerien caught a four-pound cutthroat in Gibbs once.

If you want to fish lakes year-round and regularly catch trout, there are probably no insects more important than Chironomids. Fish hit them on big water and small kettle lakes and subalpine tarns. They hatch year round, and although they are usually small, often less than a quarter-inch long, they can be very numerous. Juvenile midges come in a variety of sizes, but black, olive, brown and red seem to be the most common colors. The TDC is a good emerger, and adults can be imitated by a Griffith's Gnat. It takes a lot of patience and a long leader to fish midge pupae and larvae, but they will connect you with fish when nothing else can.

Frankly, I'd be willing to bet that more than half the trout caught by fly-fishers in Olympic Peninsula lakes are taken by people dragging a Woolly Bugger behind a float tube or boat. Depending on its color and size, a Woolly Bugger can imitate everything from a leech to a crayfish and from a dragonfly nymph to a sculpin. Three-spined sticklebacks, small schooling baitfish identifiable by their dorsal spines, aren't available in all lakes, but when they are, trout, especially cutthroat, prey on them selectively. A size 4 Woolly Bugger in black or shiny dark olive retrieved slowly through weedy shoals will often produce rattling strikes.

Dragonflies and damselfies are also a favorite diet item in lakes. In my experience, the nymphs are most effective right before and during hatches. On the peninsula, this typically occurs in late spring and early summer. Although most adult dragonflies are blue or green, the short-bodied red ones are common on some lakes, particularly Price Lake, and trout will take the adults from the surface. A dark Woolly Bugger will work as a dragonfly nymph, but an olive-bodied Carey Special is better. I like a size 10 Marabou Damselfly Nymph for the damsels.

The outlets of most low-elevation lakes on the peninsula originally connected to tidewater, and the inlets had cold water, clean gravel, and dense vegetation canopies. Lake-dwelling and sea-run cutthroat, coho, and, occasionally, sockeye spawned in the inlets, and some juvenile fish reared in the lakes. Unfortunately, the pathways to salt water have been broken on most lakes, and inlet creek spawning habitat has been degraded. But migratory fish still enter Lake Pleasant and Lake Ozette, and the resident trout in Beaver Lake and Price Lake still spawn in inlet and outlet creeks. Wild trout in these lakes, especially cutthroat, will often target fry and smolts, and a small Mickey Finn imitates them about as good as anything.

Weedy lakes, especially mid- to high-elevation lakes, occasionally contain scuds. Typically less than an inch long, these fresh water crustaceans are also available to trout year-round, usually around weed beds. They provide a high-calorie meal and are often found in great numbers. Lakes with good populations of scuds, such as the high-country's Goat Lake and Mason County's Price Lake, often turn out trout of two pounds or larger. Just about any scud pattern will work, but I have a fondness for Ted Trueblood's Trueblood Otter Shrimp. It's been around a long time, it's got all natural materials, and Trueblood was one of the last of the genuine outdoor writers.

Okay. I've left a lot of things out—most notably *Callibaetis* mayflies and the various stillwater caddis. But I believe you will catch more fish in Olympic lakes over the course of a year with these patterns than with any others.

Chapter Twenty-Five

Twenty-Five Olympic Peninsula Flies

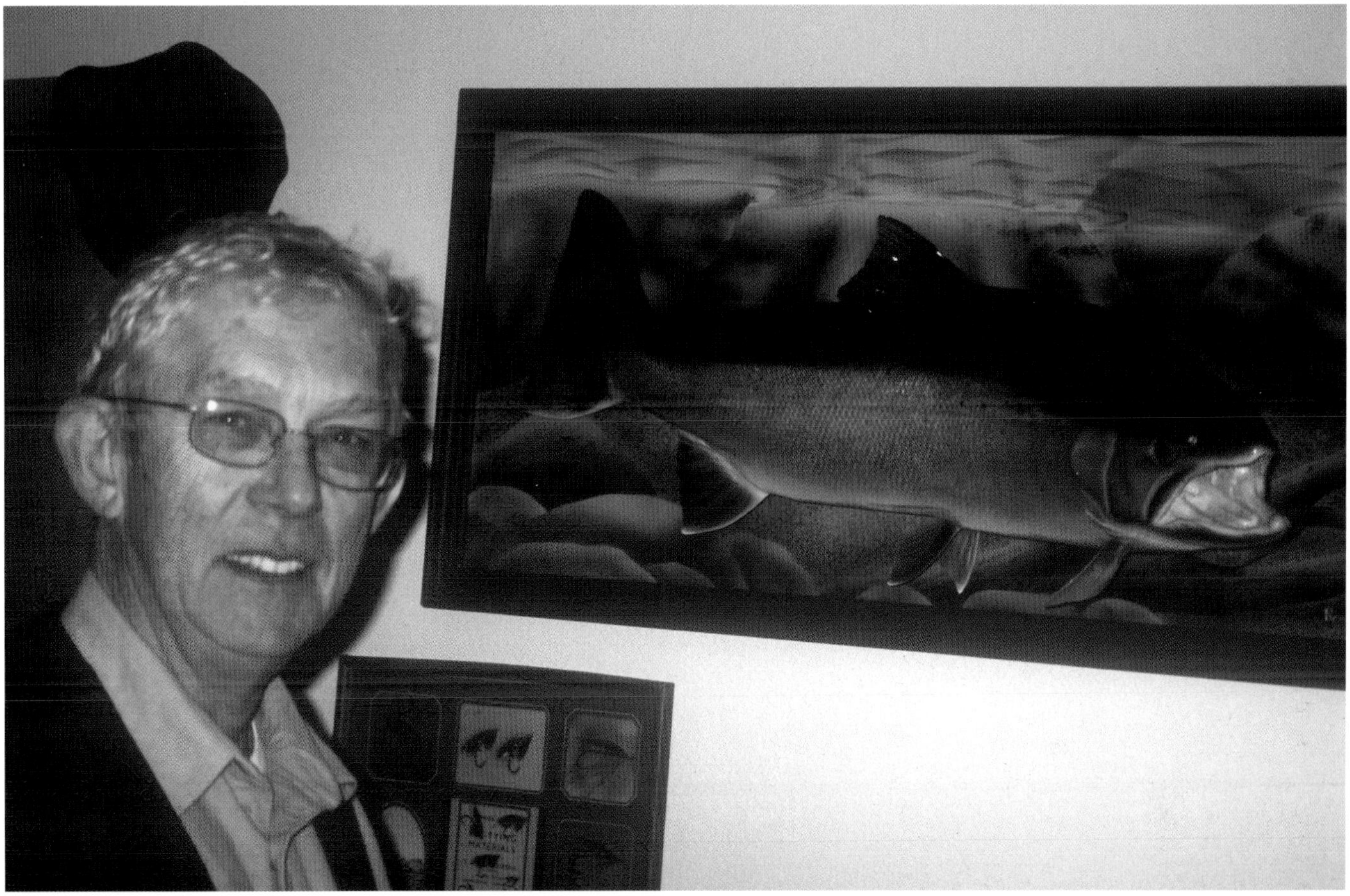

Dick Wentworth in his fly-tying room in Forks.

Wentworth Termite Fly—Dick Wentworth

In 1951, a huge wildfire swept from the upper Sol Duc, down the North Fork of the Calawah to the outskirts of Forks. "After the Forks Fire, there were a lot of snags on the sides of the hills above the Calawah," Dick said. He created this pattern to tempt the wild 5- to 6-pound summer steelhead that routinely smacked the termites that came out of the snags. "When a termite hit the water, it would go splat, splat and then wiggle."

Hook: Orvis dry-fly hook (originally made by Partridge)
Body: Silk floss or Antron, ginger or reddish brown
Wings: hackle tip, reddish brown or ginger
Hackle: brown, clipped on bottom to imitate legs

Wentworth Monster Moth—Dick Wentworth

Dick fishes this fly on Lake Crescent. Although most people fish the lake with sunken flies, Dick has taken fish to 8 pounds on dry flies.

Hook: Mustad 2X long 9671, size 2
Body: Antron yarn wound tight to create segmented look
Wing: Antron yarn, fanned out
Hackle: Badger

Kaas' Feather Duster—Don Kaas

This is a series of steelhead flies with the same profile and ingredients but different colors. Don ties it with olive wings and green body, black wings and red body and olive/red. He fishes a floating line and uses large, heavy hooks to get them to sink quickly in the broken water he prefers. "I always try to tie a fly so it gets down right away," he said. "I tie it in sections because it has more motion without so much bulk. It just pulses in the water."

Hook: Partridge Single Salmon M
Tail: ostrich, olive or black
Body: holographic tinsel, green or wine
Hackle support: peacock herl ball with olive wings, black ostrich with black wings
Hackle: grizzly hen hackle dyed olive (green wing), pheasant hackle dyed olive (green wing), guinea natural (black wing)

Sol Duc Crawdad—Don Kaas

Don takes summer steelhead and cutthroat on this pattern. "I've found crawdads in their bellies," he said. "Big cutts will hit it like a freight train. I always look for otters working a riffle for crawdads because cutthroat will hang downstream and pick up the pieces."

Hook: Partridge Single Salmon M
Body: Krystal Flash strands, green, mixed with green thread
Wing and tail: fox squirrel, natural; front and rear
Hackle: grizzly
Topping: ring-necked pheasant rump feather
Head: Cactus Chenille, small green

Meadow Hole—Don Kaas

This is named for a summer-run and cutthroat hole on the Calawah. "I use it and the Silver Hilton in the fall, and the rest of my flies just get left in the box," he said. "On the 200R hook it works just beneath the surface in tail-outs and slow water.

Hook: 200R or Gamakatsu T10-6H, 4-10 (to sink faster)
Tail: pheasant rump, dyed black
Rib: Ultra Wire, small, red
Body: peacock herl
Underwing: four peacock sword feathers
Wing: pheasant rump feather, black
Head: peacock herl

Sand Rock—Don Kaas

An elegant cutthroat and steelhead pattern for spring through late fall. Green is a productive color on the Sol Duc when the river is clear. Don named this fly for a favorite hole on the lower Sol Duc.

Hook: TMC 200R
Tail: teal
Body: rear 2/3 yellow floss with silver rib, front 1/3 yellow Cactus Chenille
Hackle: grizzly hackle (two turns), teal (two turns)
Head: peacock herl

Lab Rat—Don Kaas

You can figure out the name of this fly if you hold it vertically by the head. Don caught a 14-pound spring chinook on his third or fourth cast with it. "It about blew my mind," he said. "It came about 15 feet for the fly. I caught three or four springers on it that year."

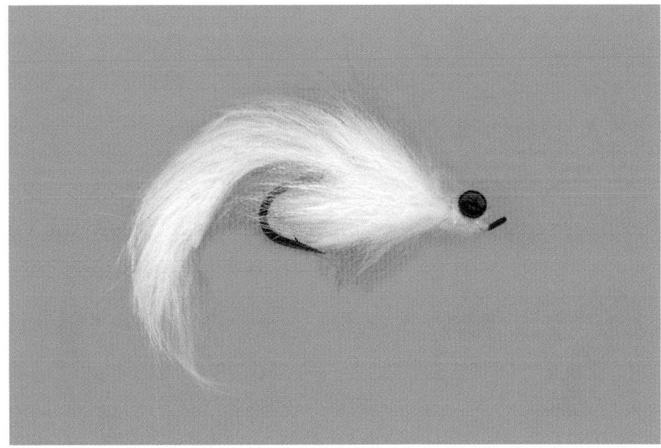

Hook: Atlantic salmon, heavy
Tail and body: rabbit, white
Head: bead chain

Garrett Ant

Carpenter ants swarm out of cedar snags during the first genuine hot spell in May or early June. According to Don Kaas, James Garrett swore by this simple ant pattern for cutthroat and steelhead when the ants were on the wing. "One time we were sitting in lawn chairs at the edge of the water at Bear Spring," he said. "He saw a steelhead and went and got a rod and cast the ant. He didn't get the cast where he wanted but the fish peeled 7 or 8 feet right to it."

Hook: TMC 3761, wet fly, size 4-8
Body: yarn, tapered, black
Hackle: black, trimmed above to form beard
Head: peacock herl, dyed black

Dungeness Silver—James Garrett

Garrett created this dressing for coho salmon when he lived at the Dungeness hatchery in the 1970s.

Hook: Atlantic salmon, heavy, 1-2/0
Body: rear half fluorescent orange yarn, front half, fluorescent yellow yarn
Rib: flat silver tinsel entire body
Wing: fluorescent yellow over fluorescent orange marabou

Gloria's Green Skirt—James Garrett

Most patterns for chum salmon in fresh water feature a lot of green, and this is no exception. Gloria was Garrett's wife.

Hook: Atlantic salmon heavy, 6-2/0
Butt: fluorescent green chenille in an egg shape
Hackle: fluorescent yellow directly in front of butt
Shoulder: fluorescent hot-orange or flame chenille in egg shape

Curt's Woven Stone—Curtis Reed

This pattern has taken many nice Elwha rainbows. Two very similar species of large "golden" stoneflies are found in Olympic Peninsula rivers—the true golden stone and the slightly smaller western stonefly. You don't have to worry about the difference if you carry this pattern in sizes 6 and 8.

Hook: TMC 5263
Tail: goose biot (small cream dubbing ball to separate tail and body optional)
Body: woven black or brown V-Rib and yellow Antron yarn
Thorax: custom blended 1/2 Golden Stone (Hareline) and 1/2 dark brown Jay Fair's
Wing case: Thin Skin, mottled oak natural
Legs: ring-necked pheasant rump
Antennae: goose biot, brown

Curt's Chameleon—Curtis Reed

This elegant hair-wing was created by Waters West's Curt Reed. The polar bear (or substitute) and peacock both look slightly different in the water than they do when dry, hence the name.

Hook: Alec Jackson Spey or Bartleet, 4-8
Rib: silver tinsel, fine
Body: floss, red; Semi-Seal dubbing, bronze peacock, tied in front to support hackle
Hackle: blue peacock neck hackle
Wing: polar bear or substitute

Optimist—John McMillan

This is my good friend, John's, inspired tribute to his father, Bill McMillan's, celebrated Winter's Hope. It has feather wings like his dad's pattern (and Spey flies), and John usually ties it on large hooks because he likes to dead-drift flies. John is an expert at reading water and uses mends to present his flies precisely to holding steelhead.

Hook: Partridge 2/0-5/0
Thread: orange
Hackle: schlappen palmered, kingfisher blue
Collar: mallard
Wing: hackle tip, hot-orange, red underwing
Bead: brass

Gypsy—John McMillan

John named this pattern after his Gordon setter, who regularly accompanies him on West End rivers and grouse coverts. Its long, webby hackles remind me of the "feathers" on a setter's legs, and its wings evoke the dog's color. It's a fine summer steelhead and cutthroat fly.

Hook: Gamakatsu T10 3H, size 8-2
Body: tinsel, gold
Hackle: schlappen gray
Wing: four grizzly hackle tips, dyed magenta

Peninsula Squid—John McMillan

As two-handed rods became popular for winter steelheading on the peninsula, anglers began to fish much larger flies, some reaching five inches. This makes sense, because West End steelhead spend more time at sea than most stocks, and larger patterns better imitate squid, shrimp and baitfish. Large bright dressings like John's shank fly are also highly visible in turbid water.

Hook: Waddington shank, 25-45mm
Tail: blue rhea or small ostrich
Body: Cactus Chenille, large, hot pink
Under wing: black marabou, with pale blue bucktail on top
Over wing: rhea or small ostrich, fuchsia
Head: black barbells

Calawah Orange—John Alevras

John created this beautiful "soft hackle" type dressing for summer steelhead and cutthroat trout on West End rivers.

Hook: Alec Jackson Spey, bronze
Rear body: tinsel, gold, oval
Body: ostrich herl, pale orange
Rear hackle: soft brown hen hackle
Front hackle: barred woodduck flank

Hoh River Claret—John Alevras

This is another of John's elegant flies for sea-run cutthroat and summer steelhead. It may be fished dead drift, greased line or with a riffled hitch.

Hook: Alec Jackson Spey Fly, bronze
Body: SLF dubbing, Number 15, fiery red brown
Hackle: Salt water/Spey hackle, claret
Wing: teal
Head: black or dark claret

Satsop Blue—Unknown

My good friend, Joe Uhlman, has taken bright coho with this marabou pattern for many years. He uses it most often on the mainstem Satsop and East Fork of the Satsop.

Hook: Gamakatsu SC 15 size 2-8
Tail and body: silver mylar tubing over thread base, tail picked out
Underwing: magenta marabou
Overwing: blue marabou, with several strands silver Krystal Flash; epoxy "baitfish" type head, with stick-on eyes

Peacock and Purple Shank Fly—Dave Steinbaugh

Although they may seem like a new phenomenon, Atlantic salmon anglers on Scottish rivers have used Waddington shanks since the 19th century. They let you fish relatively small hooks—which are more difficult for fish to get leverage on than large ones—on a fly with a large profile. Dave Steinbaugh is proprietor of Waters West Fly-fishing Outfitters in Port Angeles and one of the peninsula's most experienced steelhead guides.

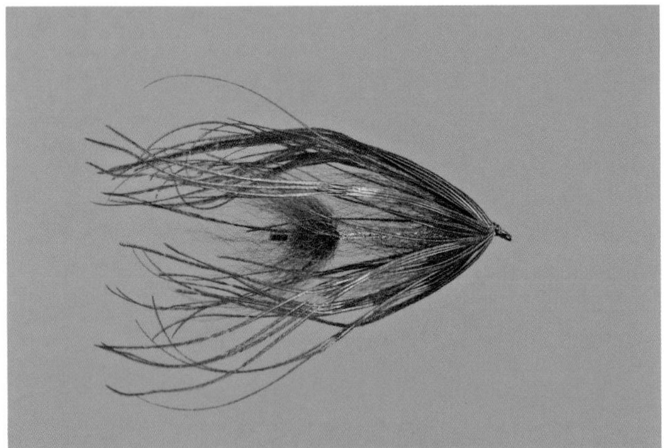

Shank: Waddington shank, 35 or 45 mm.
Hackle: eyed peacock tail, tied in by the tail
Collar: Arctic fox, purple; dubbing ball (supports collar)—seal or substitute, red

Isabella—Dave Steinbaugh

This is Dave's favorite summer steelhead Spey fly and he has used it everywhere from the West End to the Grande Ronde and Thompson.

Hook: Alec Jackson Spey 1 1/2
Tag: small oval silver tinsel
Body: purple floss over silver mylar tinsel
Rib: medium oval silver tinsel (front half of body)
Hackle: blue-eared pheasant or long webby hackle, purple
Collar: blue-eared pheasant, natural
Wing: hackle tip, black

Keta Rose—Doug Rose

This is my chum fry imitation for salt water cutthroat. It's similar to Letcher Lambuth's Candlefish, but is much more sparse and has synthetics for flash. I fish it in estuaries and along the inside of eelgrass corridors in April and May.

Hook: Gamakatsu SC 15, 4-8
Body: holographic silver tinsel
Underwing: white bucktail
Overwing: pale blue bucktail with blue Flashabou and chartreuse Angelhair
Throat: Hareline's UV minnow belly

Zostera—Doug Rose

Zostera is the taxonomic name for eelgrass, and that is where I fish this simple wet fly. I don't know why, but it is most effective on cutthroat in autumn.

Hook: Daichii 2546, sizes 4-8
Tail: root beer "mother of pearl" Gliss'n Glo
Body: silver body braid
Wing: light olive Icelandic sheep hair
Head: red thread, fairly large

Fall Surprise—George Binney

George has taken the classic Mickey Finn and forage fish color schemes, but slimmed them down and mixed them rather than tying it in layers. "These two flies have been my bread and butter for cutthroat and silvers in the salt," George says. "The Orange and Yellow Bucktail has allowed me to catch cutthroat, silvers and a steelhead all on the same tide on one day."

Hook: 200RBL, size 6
Thread: black
Body: none
Wing: orange and yellow bucktail mixed together and tied evenly around hook over gold Krystal Flash

Candlelight—George Binney

"This is my candlefish or baitfish pattern," George says. "It is similar to the Fall Surprise but there is a white bucktail throat."

Hook: 200RBL, size 6
Thread: black
Body and tail: none
Wing: four or five fibers of blue and green bucktail over green Krystal Flash
Throat: white bucktail
Topping: 4 to 6 fibers black bucktail

Andy's Stavis Bay—Ron Hirsch

Ron was shown this fly by Andy Rodgers, a Kitsap County logger and trapper who fished it on Hood Canal from the 1950s to 1970s. "He showed me this fly in 1974," Ron said. "I think it works because it's a good imitation of a herring at a critical point in the baitfish's life cycle. The loose tinsel body has flash that suggests the tiny scales of the first-year herring that become abundant in early June. If you've ever watched fish or murrelets feed on these little herring, you know their scales drop easily, and when a school is hassled, they fall like rain. No doubt, this rain of silver excites the fish."

Hook: originally a size 4-6 Roman Moser, but any heavy wet-fly hook will work
Body: silver metallic tinsel
Underwing: blue rabbit or marabou
Wing: red bucktail over several strands of metallic Flashabou

Chum Baby—Bob Triggs

Bob's chum fry pattern looks very different from mine, but it also takes a lot of salt water cutthroat. "In my area, I noticed chum fry were a ruddy brown color in early spring," Bob writes, "and they get grayish to olive color as the season progresses. I like them tied sparse, not full-bodied. Bead heads add weight and action. Unweighted, the fly works closer to the surface. I sometimes grease it with floatant and drop it near a school of bait that the cutts are actively chasing. The fly lies on or near the surface and may imitate a stunned baitfish. This seems to work better than dropping a weighted fly into the active cutts, which may be too 'invasive' an approach."

Hook: Daiichi SS number 2546, sizes 8-6
Thread: 6/0 UNI-Thread, olive
Body: Holographic mylar tinsel (silver or gold for variety)
Rib: Ultra wire, counter wrapped
Wing: fox squirrel tail (natural), spring 1- to 1 1/2 inches, increase to 2 or more inches during summer and fall. "Sometimes I add some olive color with Prisma color Pen or olive squirrel tail strands."
Collar: peacock herl. "Sometimes I extend a few herls back over the wings as a topping, and then wrap the rest of the herl as the collar. I use one piece of krystal Flash tied as a lateral line on each side of the fly, three-fourths the length of the fly."

Lily's Elwha Caddis—Ron Hirschi

I saw Ron catch a 16-inch rainbow last October from the Cable Car Hole on the middle Elwha with this fly. Although he grew up fishing for sea-run at Port Gamble, Ron spent six years in Montana and is a fine dry-fly fisherman. "I tie several versions of this fly in all the browns and greens of caddis. It mimics many species and seems to work better when shredded a few times by fish."

Hook: Dai-Riki dry fly/light nymph, 12-16
Shuck: "A generous folded gob of spring rubbed bison fur, preferably in light tan from bison that roam out of Yellowstone Park to restore life in the valleys of Wyoming and Montana. Available in pine trees along the Madison River. Or soft Antron but not so good a choice."
Body: dubbed bison soft fur or Antron in greens and browns
Wing: high floater: grizzly hackle; lower floater and sinking version: partridge or other soft hackle
Thread: "of course"

Chapter Twenty-Six

Coastal Cutthroat on the Olympic Peninsula: Blue-Backs and Yellow-Bellies

by John McMillan

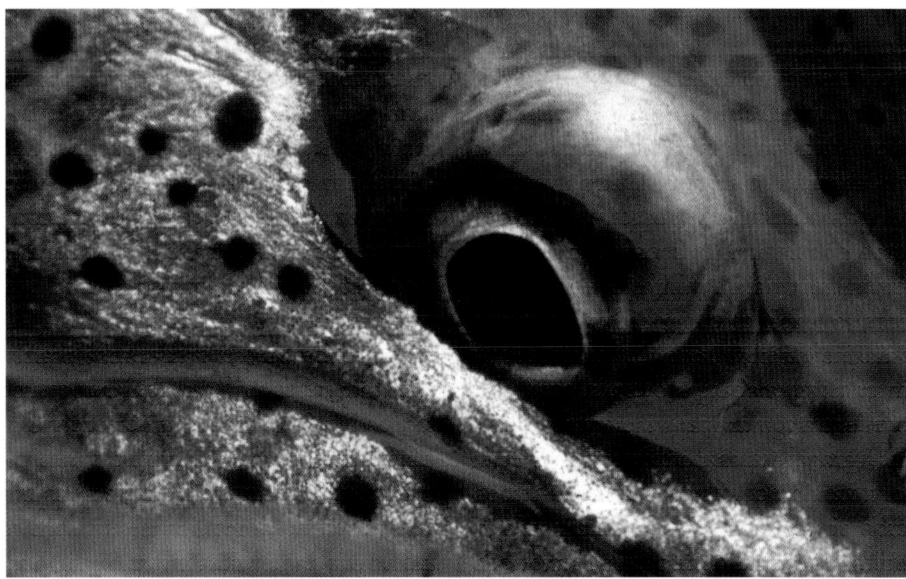

An up-close view of the incredible detail on a coastal cutthroat's head.

Coastal cutthroat were the first fish I encountered after moving to the Olympic Peninsula in 1998. I had not fished the peninsula since a summer vacation our family took there in 1984. I was 13 years old and more interested in fishing for trout in Montana and Oregon, and steelhead on Vancouver Island. I liked cutthroat well enough, but they were common on the Washougal River where I grew up. Wild Vancouver Island summer steelhead on dry flies, surface feeding Deschutes redsides, and monster Big Hole brown trout seemed more exotic.

In 1984, I landed a few cutthroat on both the Clearwater and Hoh, and noticed subtle differences in fish from each. But I could not then have imagined the interest cutthroat would stir in me later. On arriving home two weeks later, I told my friend that the peninsula was a pretty place, but I would rather vacation somewhere else in the future.

That changed when I accepted a fisheries internship during the summer of 1998 to work near Forks on the Olympic Peninsula. Based on my early memories, I thought it would be temporary until finding a job closer to summer steelhead and redsides. I fished every day after work and every weekend, hiking about 350 miles that summer up and down the famed peninsula streams. By fall, I came to realize that the rivers were more impressive than I imagined as a young boy, and unlike Montana brown trout, these fish were native and unlike the Deschutes, the rivers were not a man-made tailrace fishery.

My angling did not produce great numbers, but it did provide a window into the diversity of a Northwest Rain Forest. Although the peninsula is home to a few endemic species of plants, amphibians, and animals, I wondered why this rain forest seemed to lack the amazing diversity of fish and birds found in southern hemisphere rain forests.

I experienced a partial answer to my question one evening on a small stream. It was mid-October and large caddis were flying like drunkards—zipping, dropping, and flitting about—before briefly dapping onto the water to lay eggs. In two hours I landed several fish on skated surface flies, and shot three rolls of film. Many fish gulped at the fly multiple times, others fought for it. Some of the fish were pure silver, with soft white bellies. Others were dark brass, thick-backed fish with large, black spots, and enormous sculpted jaws. But no fish were as stunning as the few large golden-yellow fish, with tens of thousands of spots—large ovals on the back decreasing to speckled half-moons on the sides and belly.

As a friend once remarked after looking at the pictures, those fish were the "Lexus model." Indeed, they seemed crowned by the gold of Pharaohs, their jaws strong and tinged with the purest gold flake. Rain forest cutthroat are

Coastal cutthroat inhabit nearly every Olympic Peninsula creek and stream.

diversity within species, an expression of thousands of years of Olympic isolation sculpted by winter torrents, 100-year hurricane events, summer droughts, the pressure of vigilant avian fishers, and the self-driven desire of unceasing predatory instinct to consume any fish smaller than they.

I couldn't sleep that night. I drove back to the same place early the next day, but only landed a couple of fish. Perhaps they were sore-mouthed or had moved on in advance of the impending rain storm. More important was the experience of coming to realize this rain forest did indeed contain brilliant diversity. This diversity was particularly evident in the most ancient of our contemporary *Oncorhynchus* species—coastal cutthroat. After sitting on the bank for three hours, observing a pool and thinking, I drove back to town full of fresh motivation.

With my interest piqued, I sought out several people to find out if they had made similar observations. I talked to my supervisor, Phil DeCillis, a fish biologist for the USFS. I also called Warren Scarlett and Jeff Cederholm, two biologists who had lived and worked on the peninsula for over 20 years. About three weeks later, I tracked down Russ Thomas, a Forks resident who had worked in all the nearby watersheds over his long career. After numerous conversations, I came to realize that what I thought was "discovery" was, of course, already well known by scientists, anglers and locals. They recognized that cutthroat exhibited incredibly diverse morphologies, and that the patterns tended to change across rivers and seasons.

Locally, the bright cutthroat were referred to as "bluebacks" and the yellow and brassy fish were called "yellowbellies." Others denoted cutthroat as "harvest trout" or simply "natives." Some local anglers suggested the coloration variances were due to differences in river clarity, while others thought the coloration due to anadromy or residency, or that the two color types represented different runs of fish that entered streams at different times of year. Jeff and Warren provided a reasonable and insightful response: the fish were different because of their different habitat and their appearance also varied because of state of maturity.

One week later I decided I wanted to stay in Forks, and I started to look for full-time work. Outside of work, my main focus was to document differences in cutthroat morphology and life-history patterns. How quickly a mind can change. Over the next eight years I hiked and snorkeled thousands of stream miles, and catalogued thousands of photographs in hopes of increasing our understanding of the diverse coastal cutthroat.

One defining trait of coastal cutthroat is their amazing color patterns. Perhaps nowhere in Washington is this more impressive than the Olympic Peninsula. As many anglers know, cutthroat on the Hood Canal side of the peninsula often look very different from fish on the western edge of the peninsula. Furthermore, variation within a single watershed often appears to exceed that found between watersheds. For example, fish caught in small creeks often look "yellow" compared to fish caught in large rivers, which may be more "silvery" or "brassy." This raises an interesting question: Why are cutthroat so diverse in coloration and spotting?

Cutthroat coloration and spotting are fundamentally controlled by genetics, but many patterns stem from life-history strategy, proximate environmental conditions, and state of maturation. The role of these mechanisms in the coloration of cutthroat remains poorly understood, but the subject is well studied in other fish species. A review of these mechanisms can provide insight into why the "old timers" referred to cutthroat based on a color other than the red (throat) slash.

Life-history pattern is one of the most important factors affecting cutthroat coloration and spotting. We can see this clearly when comparing anadromous and resident forms. For example, all forms of cutthroat are gradations of yellow and green as juvenile parr. However, the anadromous form quickly develops gray or bluish-gray backs and silver sides and white bellies as smolts. This prepares them for the ocean environment, and can make fish nearly invisible from above. When cutthroat are in brackish water such as estuaries this silver transition can be reduced.

In contrast, fluvial and stream-resident cutthroat spend their entire lives in fresh water streams. The resident fish are often densely covered in large, black spots that sometimes run under their bellies, and their bodies are a mix of deep yellow and rich greens. The darker, naturally-blending coloration of the resident fish presumably provides them the advantage of avoiding predation and camouflaging their own predatory inclinations in fresh water environments. Coloration of the fluvial form is often intermediate between the yellow resident form and the silvery, blue-backed anadromous form.

Individual life-history color patterns may also vary between and within watersheds due to differences in proximate environmental conditions, such as light intensity. Light intensity is affected by stream canopy, instream cover, and stream turbidity. Fish coloration is determined by chromatophores, specialized cells that carry pigment of different colors. They contract and expand as fish encounter backgrounds of different colors and shifting light. This allows many fish species to change color in just 10 to 30 minutes. Consequently, we should expect fish to have different coloration and spotting patterns in different watersheds and within watersheds depending on their environment. Indeed, many anglers know this is the case.

In general, cutthroat from glacially-tinted rivers are more silvery, or pale, and have relatively sparse and faded spotting patterns, regardless of whether the fish is

A blue-back cutthroat, fresh the salt.

The golden sheen of an autumn yellow-belly

anadromous or resident. This is because turbidity reduces light penetration into the water column. In contrast, cutthroat from rain-fed systems with low turbidity levels, clear water, and high light levels exhibit more yellows and greens, with dense black spots. Similarly, fish from small tributaries with extensive canopy cover are often dark in coloration, appearing almost black in some cases. All of these differences can be explained by variations in light intensity.

Seasonal differences in light intensity also affect cutthroat. For example, cutthroat coloration during or immediately after floods is often milky and washed-out, because of reduced light intensity through the elevated turbidity. In addition, fish caught during winter are paler than fish caught during summer, although the differences are less noticeable in glacial streams.

Perhaps most remarkable is the coloration plasticity that cutthroat demonstrate over relatively short time periods. An individual moving into a rain-fed tributary from a glacial river, or vice versa, can change colors within 10 to 30 minutes depending on the conditions. The changes are sometimes so dramatic that an angler would not recognize the same fish even if it was caught before and moving into the tributary. Coloration can also vary within the same pool. Those hiding in the dark cover of logjams are substantially darker than individuals feeding near the surface in well-lighted pools.

The coloration change appears to take place more slowly when fish are entering rivers on their anadromous return, in which case individuals may retain their silvery coloration for several days, while acclimating to the new environment. The period may be shortened in places with or during times of high light intensity. There is a selective advantage in being able to change color quickly, especially in a fish like cutthroat that often rely on a variety of habitats to carry out their life cycle. Just ask the chameleon.

State of maturation can profoundly influence color, and this is well documented in many salmonid species. Like other species, male cutthroat develop vivid colors and darker spots to attract females and intimidate male competitors just before and during spawning. Females tend to undergo a similar change, although the extent is not as great as their male counterparts. Following spawning, fish tend to revert to more subdued coloration because the cost of expending energy on a secondary sexual characteristic exceeds the benefit as they recover from spawning.

When considering these factors, it is easy to imagine an anadromous fish entering a river in early October silvery and blue; shifting to a more washed-out state during early winter; darkening to rich and vibrant coloration during spawning; then reverting to less striking colors in post-spawn condition during the spring. Then the cycle starts again, with an individual either remaining in fresh water with its green and yellow, or changing again to the silver and blue for another marine visit.

It seems clear that the terms "blue-back" and "yellow-belly" refer to variations in coloration and spotting patterns that are largely due to life history, life stage, and environment. I now know the fish I landed during my serendipitous evening were a mixture of anadromous, fluvial, and resident forms in various life stages. However, all I remember are the morphological patterns and the amazing level of diversity of cutthroat in a rather short stretch of stream.

In my thirty-two years of angling, I have not stumbled upon any other group of fish that has so profoundly influenced my life. The diversity of names for cutthroat is almost equal to their morphological diversity, and I am only another in a long line of anglers who have found solace in this trout of many colors.

That cutthroat are diverse on the Olympic Peninsula is true. This means that angling provides not only a chance to catch trout, but also the opportunity to enjoy some of the finest diversity any rain forest in the world has to offer. In a single day, one can fish for stream-resident yellow-bellies in tannic creeks and small streams, and then chase larger fluvial fish in the mainstem rivers. Or, an angler could choose to fish the Hood Canal area, which may support the greatest diversity on the peninsula. One may also decide to fish for the indigenous adfluvial cutthroat of the rain forest that have been long locked behind an earthen dam—the thick-bodied *Crescenti* cutthroat of Lake Crescent. The opportunities are as broad as the diversity.

With this opportunity comes our angling responsibility to conserve these beautifully diverse fish. Coastal cutthroat are aggressive feeders. This means they are particularly vulnerable. Research indicates that mortalities on feeding trout are much higher than those found in salmon and steelhead, which typically do not feed after entering fresh water. For example, some mortality estimates are greater than 30 percent with artificial lures, and nearly all exceed the 10 percent expected for steelhead.

Fishing pressure on the Olympic Peninsula will only continue to increase over the next 20 years. Additionally, cutthroat abundance may decrease as global climate change further impacts their habitat. Consequently, it is important to consider that during summer months cutthroat are especially susceptible to angling mortality during periods of warm water. Ample research indicates that fishing for trout in water 70 degrees and above results in higher mortalities. I personally choose to quit fishing at temperatures above 67 degrees.

While I have not arrived at any extraordinary cutthroat conclusions, I have come to realize that Jeff and Warren were largely right. While I would like to think my photographs have contributed to understanding the relationship between their morphology, life history, and environment, as with most scientific or impassioned endeavors, I remain with more questions than answers. But there is more intrigue and hope than I started with.

Chapter Twenty-Seven

Rivers of Sand

by Ron Hirschi

Boulders, sand, gravel and blow down are the building blocks of cutthroat beaches.

When I first discovered what they were in technical terms, I remembered childhood fishing trips to places now more precisely defined with a new brand of ecological jargon: Drift cells. Okay. I remember. These are the places that provide my favorite fishing on the planet, for sea-run cutthroat trout. But what's all the fuss about these drift cells? Haven't they been there all along? Long before they had defining nomenclature didn't we recognize their functions, their values? It was probably in the summer of 1960 when I first fell into the search pattern I've maintained since catching my first cutthroat and nice coho at a place we called "The Point." I rowed my little boat over to the point to fish all summer long. In those days, my go-to gear was a lightweight spinning rod and wobbly abalone lure that was dynamite. I would anchor and spend lots of time with my head over the gunnels, admiring the swarms of new herring and clouds of what I called "candlefish," now usually referred to as sand lance.

I'd cast and retrieve, catching fat coho and slender cutthroat at the tip of the point. Tidal water rushed up from the bay to the south or swirled in from bigger waters to the north. If I had the time, I also rowed to another "point" and fished to my heart's content, imagining that everybody else on the planet had the same wondrous places to enjoy. Little did I know how lucky I was to be living in the Pacific Northwest at a time when almost no one fished in the salt for trout. My Uncle Chuck was one of the few who did and when he inquired about my fishing success, he'd ask if I got them at "The Point," shifting his eyes from east to west, clearly defining which of the points he meant.

For some inexplicable reason, I soon switched over to flies for trout and have spent many days lobbing baitfish imitations to swirls along the drift cells of Hood Canal and the easter straits. What I fell into by default so many years ago has now become a mantra for me when talking about finding fish along marine shorelines and about protecting the integrity of drift cells. My words simply echo many years of following the path of the cells to find fish. Those paths usually, but not always, end up at points where fishing can be the very best.

At first glance, drift cells are simple constructs. At their upper ends, a classic cell begins with high bluffs. Trees, rocks and soil fall from the face of these cell-feeding bluffs onto a beach. All this eroded mass might heap up and remain, except for the winds that blow up and down our coastlines throughout the year.

Eroding bluffs can line the entire path of many cells, but they typically taper down to a more gentle slope, even giving way to marshy flats or sweeping into a bay in a modified point that hooks to enclose an estuary. As wind-driven waves pick up steam and carry the sand and other debris, some of the transported matter drops out. A net flow of sand, trees and stones moves along the length of a given cell, depositing the contents all along the way. Eventually, the deposition ends at some point, often at those places we have chosen to call just that. Picture a river of sand and debris moving along the beach and you can easily imagine how a drift cell works. Walk a beach near a prominent point in winter and you may see the erosion and deposition in action if the wind is fierce and the waves are pounding the shore. In some places it is not uncommon to have virtually all the sand stripped from a beach one day and returned the next.

I think of drift cells as rivers of sand, but these days anything from tennis balls to broccoli spears are carried along the beach. Big logs were once a major part of the action, but they have given way to sawn logs and much smaller trees and shrubs that topple onto the beach. If the beach has little or no shoreline modification, the drift cell creates a rather distinct segment along the shore. It has a beginning, where the trees and sand fall, a middle section, where all moves like a river, and a terminal location that could become a prized fishing location.

The terminus of the cell always ends where wind drops off for some reason. A headland might jut out into the waterway. A river delta or bay can end a cell. Some other land features might also create a situation where north winds predominate along a given stretch of shoreline then south wind-driven sand meets the same precise "point." Here is where you will find those beautifully designed shoreline features we give names to—Brown's Point, Green Point, Point No Point, Marrowstone Point, Point Hudson. You get my point. These cuspate, or "tooth-shaped", points are prominent along the shore where a drift cell originating from one wind direction collides with a drift cell that originates from the opposite wind direction.

The worst thing to happen to drift cells is the armoring or banks by humans since the earliest days on non Indian settlement. The key here is that a natural cell has a sort of balanced movement of sand along the entire length of beach. In that sand, baitfish, including smelt and sand lance, lay their eggs. When bulkheads line the shore, sand does not move quite as it should. The beach coarsens from lack of sand or from modified wave actions. Sadly, we have now chronicled the loss of mile after mile of baitfish spawning habitat. That loss is a key factor in sportfish declines and has even diminished the food sources of humpbacked whales, once the most common large whale of Puget Sound. Trout and salmon may still lurk along the drift cells in ways they always have done, but their prey is not as abundant. Still, you can use the cell as a pathway to find precise points at which fish will be waiting for the real thing, or any imitation. Another key feature of the cell is that eelgrass beds and other algal communities take root or hold tight to the sand and other materials carried along the cell's path. If the right balance of sediment settles, eelgrass can take root and thrive. Armor too heavily and eelgrass roots can be torn from the sea floor.

You can fish the length of a cell, enjoying the rich fish and invertebrate communities along an eelgrass-rich shoreline. Eelgrass will be dense within the midsection of a drift cell and in the bays where cells typically start and stop. These seagrass meadows might offer fishing opportunities all year long. But learn where and when to toss a fly on the downwind side of a point and you can find predictable fishing in water that often feels like your favorite pool in your favorite river. Find any small blip in the shoreline where big rocks push the dift cell away from the ordinary path. Here is where you will also find cutthroat waiting for a fly, as if lying in wait in a stream's best log jam.

As if this was not already programmed enough for those of us who wish to fish, juvenile salmon also follow the path of drift cell. Chum are especially tuned to life in drift cells. They outmigrate along the shore, literally falling into drift cells as if tiny pieces of sand dropping onto the beach from a feeder bluff. No bigger than the end of your index finger, baby chum move along the shore in inches-deep water, collecting in large numbers within drift cell terminal areas. They might swirl into the mouth of a small estuary at the tip of a small sand spit. They might also congregate at both the beginning and end zones of a drift cell, caught in the tug of wind-driven waves and tide surges.

Herring and sand lance are probably less involuntary than chum in the drift cell river, but they definitely move into cells. Points are especially promising places to find large concentrations of these baitfish. I have walked the final two miles of a local drift cell, trying to count sand lance. Let's just say I always give up and simply say there were two miles of sand lance terminating at, you guessed it, "The Point."

So now you can read the shoreline as I did when I was a kid and walk beaches as I do now. When you do, find yourself a favorite point, then gaze up the shoreline to see where the sand that created this shoreline feature came from. Scout the pathway of the cell and you will find several minor points where fish congregate. If you spend enough time along the shore, you might find some ways to restore the functions of the cell of your choosing. There are hundreds of these unique segments circling the Olympic Peninsula. Scout them like you would your favorite stream. Enjoy their diverse forms. Chances are good you will discover a point all your own.

Chapter Twenty-Eight

Beaver Ponds

Beaver dams can be found on the tidewater portions of some Hood Canal creeks.

The last trout I caught before the conclusion of the traditional river season one October came from a beaver pond. It was a brook trout, an easy 15 inches, and as fat as a vicar. In its spawning dress, with its shimmery black back and white fin tips, its splashes of orange and blue, and vivid red spots, it was a perfect Halloween fish. It hit a bright nymph, a Lightning Bug. For a moment or two I thought I would lose it; as is the case on many beaver ponds, the shoreline of this pond is a tangle of stick-ups, mud and submerged logs, and savvy fish know how to break you off. I lose more large fish on it than I catch.

The pond is about a half mile from one of Hood Canal's major rivers, and only about a quarter mile from the road. Curiously, I have never seen any evidence that anyone else fishes it. There is no trash around it, no tangles of monofilament or nightcrawler tubs, and I never see any footprints in the ankle-deep mud that surrounds much of the pond. This strikes me as peculiar, because it is an easy hike into it, unlike the routes to most beaver ponds.

I think I know why no one else fishes the pond: It simply doesn't look like it would contain trout. It is big enough, more than an acre at high water, about two-thirds that in autumn. But it is bordered by mud and sedges and blowdown, and the pond itself is cross-hatched by snags. It looks more like a seasonal wetland than a trout pond. From the woods above it, you would mistake it for one of those warm, shin-deep potholes that are scattered throughout the eastern Olympics. There's one just like it a few miles down the road, and it doesn't have trout.

You need to hike down to the pond to understand why the fish thrive in it. Several seeps and springs on the hillsides above the pond and a hop-over tributary pour cold water into it year round. The pond remains dark green and cool, with no scum on the water, even in September. If you climb up the big rock, on its south side, you will notice the course of a deeper channel through the middle of the pond, probably the relict channel of an old tributary. I wouldn't doubt if there are springs on the bottom, too. Mayflies, midges, caddisflies, dragonflies and damsels hover over the water. It's a gem.

Now, I'm something of a nut on the subject of beaver ponds. The opening day of the river season in June usually finds me on one, and I often end the season with them.

I spend a lot of time analyzing maps and talking to people about potential ponds. A few years ago, my wife and Lily and I wandered the woods near Port Ludlow every Saturday for weeks trying to locate a pair of ponds. We eventually found them, but one had dried up and the other was literally covered with lily pads. That's standard. Beaver ponds come and go. They dams blow out during winter storms or they gradually turn into marsh. I believe the word Ephemeroptera should apply as much to beaver ponds as to mayflies.

But I've found some dandies. Last fall I celebrated the 20th anniversary of discovering a pond on a tributary to the Big Quilcene. I caught my biggest brookie on it, a three-pounder that I could barely get my hands around, and many wild cutthroat over 15 inches. I used to fish a pond on tidewater where you could catch sea-bright cutts a tide change from Hood Canal on one cast, and amber-flanked, dark-backed resident fish on the next.

Beaver ponds are located all around the peninsula, but you have to work to find them. Regional fish or wildlife biologists will occasionally give you a heads-up on the general location of ponds. Some salmon restoration and fish habitat reports also document areas with ponds. Otherwise, start with a topographical map for an area that you believe could have beaver ponds. They are usually in flat areas, where the contour lines are far apart. Look for little blue splotches of water that are surrounded by the symbols for marsh or trees. When you find something promising, call the courthouse and ask if they have aerial photos for the area. Aerial photos aren't infallible, because dams blow out and ponds dry up. But if you see a pond, it's time to get out the hiking boots.

Cutthroat and brookies are the most common species in ponds. My favorite beaver pond fly is probably a Zug Bug, although anything with a peacock herl body works fine. Damselfly nymphs are usually productive in the early season, and Gold Ribbed Hare's Ears and Prince Nymphs are good when mayfly nymphs are active. I have caught a lot of beaver pond trout on small black Woolly Buggers and soft hackles. I don't fish dry flies much, but Les Johnson has been doing it longer than I have, and he says they are his favorite flies for beaver ponds. Some of my largest beaver pond trout have hit weighted Spruce flies, and I watched Curtis Reed take a 16-incher last spring from the pond at the beginning of the story with a Ruby Leech.

Ultimately, I think beaver pond fishing is like eating raw oysters—you either like it immediately or you never will. I have taken friends to my ponds over the years. They have all caught nice trout, and I thought they had enjoyed themselves, but Ron Hirschi is the only one who has ever wanted to return to one. That's probably partly due to the fact that they are tough places to cast. Anglers used to fishing from boats or large rivers are frequently driven mad by the hardhack and tules and cattails that usually provide a casting backdrop on beaver ponds. Moreover, the bottoms of most beaver ponds are soft, preventing you from wading. With their muck and snags and cedar-stained water, beaver ponds aren't the kinds of places that end up in fly-fishing art or on magazine covers, either.

Robert Traver, author of the classic Michigan fly-fishing book *Trout Madness* loved beaver ponds as much as anyone: "Perhaps it is only one man's small rebellion against this whole tedious bigger-and-better philosophy as it more and more afflicts our outdoors, indeed our very life . . ."

Sea-run cutthroat can easily negotiate beaver dams.

Chapter Twenty-Nine

Chinook on the Fly

John McMillan wading deep to present his fly.

I got into the habit of stopping into Waters West Fly-fishing Outfitters in Port Angeles on Sunday mornings. The store is quiet then and I had a chance to talk with Dave Steinbaugh, the store's owner.

"I got a chinook this morning," Dave said one drizzly Sunday. "On the Hoh." Dave said it casually, like you would say "I saw some elk on the Hoh this morning."

"This morning?" I asked. It was just a little after 11 o'clock.

"Yeah, I drove out early. I landed a 20-pounder and a bigger one got away."

"On your Spey rod?"

Dave nodded. "On a big, purple Egg Sucking Leech."

Now, it's about an hour and a half, at least, to the Hoh from P.A. and the store opens at 11 on Sundays. That gives you an idea of what time Dave set the alarm for the night before.

The point is that Dave knew it was time to try for a chinook. After one of the driest autumns in memory, when low water had kept both chinook and coho in the ocean weeks after their normal river entry timing, we had finally had a real bringing-the-mallards-down-from-Alaska storm. That was earlier in the week, and the Hoh had time to drop back into shape. Sunday morning was the moment, the best time of the entire year, for a bright fall chinook. The very best anglers feel these moments in their bones and act on them without thinking.

Knowing when to hit the water is important for chinook, the largest and strongest Pacific salmon, because they prefer deep, turbulent holding water once they get very far above the reach of the tide. Unless the weather is cooperative—sullen skies and drizzle are best—they can quickly become dour. But fish fresh from the ocean are still usually aggressive and can be found in pools, even tidewater flats, where you can reach them. You cast and strip the fly through the water and the kings will occasionally even chase it.

Of the three races native to the Olympic Peninsula, you have the best odds of taking a fall chinook on a fly. The only springer stock with an open season is the Sol Duc's, and they are notoriously close-mouthed. Summer and spring/summer fish are available in more rivers, but Queets summer chinook haven't been open for a long time, and you have to hire a tribal guide to fish the lower Quinault. That leaves the Hoh, Quillayute and Sol Duc stocks, and fly-fishers don't catch a lot of them either. Fall chinook, which usually arrive in August or later, are the most widespread and most abundant. They spawn in everything from the Hoko to the Hoquiam, but the bulk of them are taken in the Hoh, Sol Duc, Quillayute and Humptulips.

Dave's choice of the Hoh made sense. Its lower reaches are accessible all the way to tidewater, and it turns out the second most fall fish, behind the Sol Duc. The Sol Duc doesn't have as much prime chinook fly-water as the Hoh, although the Quillayute does when the water is up. The Quillayute also has plenty of access. The Queets turns out most of its chinook on the lower drift, from Hartzell Creek boat ramp down to the Clearwater Bridge takeout.

The best presentation for chinook is deep and slow, giving the fish a long look at it. You can accomplish this with a single rod if you are in a boat and have someone work the oars for you. But if you are wading—and especially if you are above tidewater—you will have much better luck with a two-handed rod. Chinook often want a big offering and larger rods let you cast much larger flies and the heavy tips you need to get them down. Equally important, 12- to 15-foot rods allow you to use mending and rod control to hang the fly in the depths for as long as possible.

The mail-order fly catalogs offer a number of flies for chinook, but the purple Egg Sucking Leech is as good as any. However, long-time Port Angeles fly-fisher and innovative and talented tier, Don Kaas, has created a similar pattern that has worked extremely well on the traditionally dour Sol Duc springers. It is also a rabbit leech, but instead of black or purple it is brilliant white. The long white body and black-painted lead eyes suggested the name Don gave it—the Lab Rat.

"I got a fish with it on the Sol Duc on about my third cast," Don said. "I got it at the boat launch at the hatchery. I saw a fish and cast to it, but another came out of nowhere and charged about 15 feet and took it. I've never seen that before. I got three or four of them that year on that fly."

You can try to duplicate Don's feat at the ramp, but there are plenty of other places above tidewater to try on the Hoh and Quillayute and Sol Duc. John McMillan has snorkeled just about every inch of the West End rivers, and he knows where the big kings like to hang out.

"They are definitely around log jams and in canyons on the Hoh," he said. "On the Hoh, they like the canyons for the cover and for the recharge from groundwater that keeps the temperature down. But on the Sol Duc they like different water. You tend to see them in slots off to the side of faster water. They like the seams off scour pools. I think you've got to see them and it helps to catch moving fish. I do best at dusk."

Chapter Thirty

Saltwater Cutthroat Diet

Ron Hirschi fishing Dabob Bay during the chum fry migration.

Ron Hirschi and I conduct a couple of salt water fly-fishing clinics each year, and the high point of the day occurs when we seine several beaches with Ron's net. Ron is a fisheries biologist and has done extensive seining along Olympic Peninsula waters to document the movements and distribution of juvenile salmon and other species. The seining in our clinics gives fly-fishers a chance to see the creatures that are important in the diet of cutthroat in salt water. People have been doing this sort of thing for years with insects in rivers, and we thought it would be a good idea to offer it in the salt. After we seine, we talk about the life histories of the creatures we have collected and the flies and presentations that imitate them.

Several years ago, we did our first haul at Cline Spit, the boat launch on Dungeness Bay. When I was caretaker at Dungeness National Wildlife Refuge, I frequently saw cutthroat working the nearshore shallows in early spring. I assumed most were feeding on chum and pink fry from the Dungeness River, but I figured they must also feed on juvenile surf smelt from time to time. Smelt spawn in the fine sand and crushed shell at the high-tide line all around Dungeness Harbor and Dungeness Spit, and juveniles that hatch in early winter are approximately two inches long by spring—a perfect size for foraging cutthroat.

Ron and I lucked out that morning. When we flipped the net over, it contained a handful of shimmering, translucent fish. They were about the length of your little finger, with large black eyes.

"Look," Ron said, to the dozen anglers in waders gathered around the seine. "Those are smelt. Juvenile surf smelt."

The net also contained 1 1/4- to 2-inch chum and pink salmon fry, juvenile sculpin, and a few broken-backed shrimp. After that, we drove over to Port Williams and hiked down Gibson Spit toward the mouth of Sequim Bay.

Cutthroat forage along the flooded edges of pickleweed and saltgrass during high tides.

We took two hauls along the gravel beach, between the beach and the eelgrass. We found crago and broken-backed shrimp, staghorn sculpins, some larger smelt, as well as the guaranteed crowd-pleasers, pipefish, the north Pacific's counterpart of sea-horses. It was nearly low tide by the time we reached the mouth of the bay and the Bell Creek lagoon was dry except for a trickle from the creek. We found more chum and coho, juvenile sculpins, and first- and second-year three-spined sticklebacks.

All of this is fascinating, but it doesn't do you much good as a fly-fisher unless you know which of these creatures cutthroat actually eat, and when they are available. Other than recent limited studies of Hood Canal and the Pacific Ocean there was little scientific information on what cutthroat actually eat in salt water. Moreover, although you could still kill cutthroat in Puget Sound until the 1990s, most anglers don't seem to have paid much attention to the fish's stomach contents. Fly-fishers seemed to assume that herring and shrimp accounted for the bulk of a sea-run's diet in tidewater, and traditional salt water cutthroat fly patterns reflected the conventional wisdom. Dressings that weren't simple attractor patterns tended to imitate herring and shrimp, occasionally sculpins.

That all changed with the publication of "Diet Items of Cutthroat in South Puget Sound" in 2001 by Joe Jaquet, a biologist with the Washington Department of Fish and Wildlife. I heard about Joe's research through the grapevine, but it took me quite a while to locate the report. As a long-time salt water cutthroat angler—and part-time cutthroat guide—I was very interested in learning what cutthroat eat during their tidewater sojourns. Like most salt water anglers, I have experienced days when cutts were feeding all around me and I couldn't find anything to tempt them. But I must admit that I wasn't prepared for some of the findings in Joe's report.

The most useful thing I learned was the importance of chum fry in the diets of salt water cutts, especially large fish. According to Joe's research, cutthroat prey very heavily on chum fry in estuaries and nearshore migratory corridors during March and April. Unlike coho and steelhead, which rear for extended periods in fresh water, chum (and pink) fry drop down to tidewater immediately after emerging from the gravel in spring. This makes them available to the cutthroat that return to salt water during early spring after wintering or spawning in rivers. Fly-fishers such as Haig-Brown were aware of the importance of juvenile chum and pink salmon in the lower reaches of rivers, and his Silver Lady was created to imitate fry. But I had never seen anything that suggested their importance to cutthroat along salt water beaches.

Since I read Joe's report, I have caught a lot more nice cutthroat off river mouths and in the shallows between the eelgrass and the gravel in springtime. I nearly always fish a simple bucktail of mine, the Keta Rose. It is similar to Letcher Lambuth's Candlefish, with a pale blue over white bucktail wing and traces of chartreuse Angel Hair and a few strands of Hareline's UV Minnow Belly for a throat. The Minnow Belly suggests the pearly white shimmer of a fry's belly, and I believe it may be a trigger to cutts. I have heard that the backs of Puget Sound chum fry are more green/olive than blue, and my friend, Bob Triggs' highly successful pattern, the Chum Baby, has an olive-brown back.

The most surprising thing in Joe's report was the salt water cutthroat's appetite for polychaete worms. It shouldn't have surprised me because Les Johnson wrote about trolling "sand worms" for cutts off Redondo in *Sea-Run* 30 years ago, but I had simply forgotten about it. Joe found that cutthroat over 12 inches feed on worms consistently and throughout the year. It isn't hard to see why. Ranging from 2 to more than 18 inches, and approaching the girth of a garter snake, polychaetes pack a lot of meat on them. Polychaetes spend most of their time on the bottom, but they engage in after-dark mating "swarms" on the surface during spring. A friend of mine witnessed this once and said large cutthroat would dash into the swarm, bite a worm in half, and then circle back to pick off the pieces—just like chinook on herring.

Speaking of herring, there were surprisingly few in the stomachs of South Sound cutthroat stomachs. There were also few sand lance or surf smelt, although quite a few "unidentified" fish were recorded. By weight, seven diet items accounted for 83 percent of the stomach contents; in descending order, they were: chum eggs and fry, polychaete worms, shiner perch, shrimp, amphipods, and herring. Although isopods and amphipods topped the list, they were consumed largely by smaller fish. The report also indicated that, contrary to my notions, cutthroat preyed significantly on bottom-dwelling organisms. Besides polychaetes, they fed on clam necks and arrow gobies, a small bottomfish that is often found near the openings of mud shrimp burrows.

The absence of forage fish seemed odd to me, but I attributed it the sea-runs' well-known tendency to feed opportunistically. The five fingers of lower Puget Sound are full of mud flats, with mile upon mile of polychaete habitat, and it's also home to the region's most productive chum runs. I figured herring, sand lance and surf smelt would have a much more prominent place in the menu of cutthroat to the north, and a couple of years ago the King County Department of Natural Resources released a study that confirmed my suspicions. Its "Nearshore Dietary Habits of Juvenile Salmon and Cutthroat Trout" found that adult cutthroat of all sizes ate herring more frequently than any other species and by quite a wide margin.

Neither of these reports studied Olympic Peninsula cutthroat, but I believe the cutthroat that roam Hood Canal, Admiralty Inlet and the eastern Strait of Juan de Fuca feed like both north and south Puget Sound fish. Olympic Peninsula waters contain the most extensive forage fish

Sea-run cutthroat encounter three-spined sticklebacks in estuaries during August and September.

spawning grounds in the state. Ribbons of chum fry migrate along nearshore beaches during springtime, and I've seen cutthroat slashing through schools of juvenile herring, sandlance and surf smelt many times in June. Broken-back and crago shrimp, amphipods and isopods are abundant in protected waters, and many bays and lagoons contain huge colonies of polychaetes. An earlier study of Hood Canal cutthroat identified gammarid amphipods as the most important diet item there, followed by Callianasid shrimp (mud shrimp), isopods, sand lance, and chum fry (11 percent).

As with most teaching endeavors, Ron's and my seining clinics have probably helped us more than the clients. They give us an idea what's in the water, and where and when. The new reports have provided invaluable information on what the cutthroat are looking for, and which flies we should use. Ultimately, it's all conjecture and extrapolation, just as in figuring out which insects trout are feeding on in rivers. That's part of the charm of fly-fishing. But at least we feel like we are fishing more intelligently now—if not exactly always successfully.

Crago shrimp with eggs in spring.

Juvenile sculpins taken from the Bell Creek estuary in April.

Juvenile shiner perch are abundant in protected bays during May.

Amphipods provide a year-round food source for cutthroat in nearsore waters.

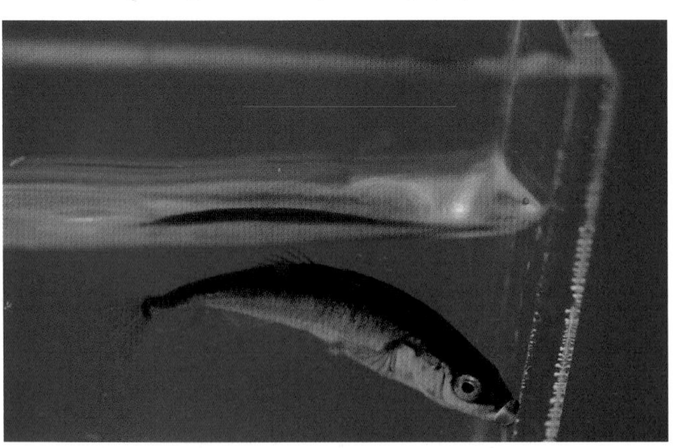

First-year three-spined sticklebacks.

Surf smelt, chum fry and stickleback taken in one haul from Dungeness Bay in spring.

APPENDIX

Fly Shops

Waters West Fly-fishing Outfitters (Port Angeles): 360-417-0937, www.waterswest.com. Waters West's proprietor Dave Steinbaugh has created one of the West Coast's best fly shops. In addition to standard fly tackle, it has an extensive selection of Spey rods and reels, Spey and salt water tying materials and flies, guide service, and clinics on everything from Spey casting to fly tying and salt water cutthroat. It sells many local patterns, including the Sol Duc Spey, flies by John Alevras, Bob's Possum Stone, and Don Kaas's Lab Rat, Sand Rock and Meadow Hole.

Port Townsend Angler: 360-379-3763. A surprising amount of tackle, flies and materials are tucked into this small Port Townsend fly shop. It is located near the northeast Olympics' popular lowland lakes and salt water beaches, and features productive local flies such as Bob Triggs' Chum Baby, Jim Kerr's Jim Dandy, and proprietor, Mike Duncan's, creations. Guide service.

Traditional Sporting Goods Stores: These shops usually have limited selections of fly-fishing gear but you can often find leaders and tippet and other things you need. They also usually have good information on river conditions and whether fish are around.

Forks: Olympic Sporting Goods, 360-374-6330
Thriftway, 360-374-6161

Port Angeles: Swains General Store, 360-452-2357

Sequim: Swains Outdoor, 360-681-6561

Port Townsend: Swains Outdoor, 360-385-1313

Shelton: Verles, 360-426-0933

Elma: The Dennis Company, 360-482-2321

Montesano: The Dennis Company, 360-249-4821

Aberdeen: Failor's Sporting Goods, 360-533-3762

Maps

Olympic National Forest/Olympic National Park: This is the basic planimetric map—meaning it depicts the world as "flat," with no topography—for the area. It identifies major roads, rivers, most lowland lakes, and campgrounds. Available at National Park and National Forest offices, most outdoor-oriented stores, and Waters West.

Department of Natural Resources Public Land Quadrangles: These are also planimetric but are more detailed, and include smaller bodies of water and more roads, especially log roads. They also detail public and private property ownership boundaries. Maps that cover the peninsula—Cape Flattery, Forks, Copalis Beach, Mount Olympus, Port Angeles, Port Townsend, Shelton and Seattle. Available at the Forks Thrifty Mart (not all) and from the DNR at www.dnr.wa.gov/dataandmaps.

Custom Correct Maps: Manufactured by a Port Angeles company, Custom Correct maps are topographical maps (they depict elevation contours) that focus on a specific area popular with hikers rather than the arbitrary grids of USGS topos. They are convenient because you can carry one map if you are, say, hiking into Seven Lakes Basin rather than several, which is often the case with other maps. These maps also have accurate mileage distances at regular intervals for the trails. Because they cover fairly large areas, they have less detail than USGS quads. Available at most ranger stations, outdoor shops, and Waters West. Information on how to order online is available at www.customcorrectmaps.com.

USGS 7.5 Minute Quadrangle Maps: These are the classic pale green topographical maps that outsdoorsmen have used for decades. They have excellent detail and will often reveal small features of rivers such as sloughs and islands that other maps omit. They are also good in locating areas with beaver ponds. As mentioned above, the problem with USGS maps is that rivers, lakes, and trails often "run off" the corners of a map, requiring you to buy two or three different quads for a small area. It takes a long time to order the maps so it's best to buy them locally. They are available at Sport Townsend (360-379-9711) in Port Townsend and Browns (360-457-4150) in Port Angeles.

Washington River Maps & Fishing Guide: (Frank Amato Publications). This large-format publication contains maps of all the major rivers in Washington and shows boat ramps, run timing of fish, productive fly-fishing techniques, and information on campgrounds, RV parks, hotels, and Chambers of Commerce. It includes the Quillayute rivers, Hoh, Queets, Quinault, Chehalis, Humptulips, Wynoochee, Satsop, Hoko/Pysht, Elwha, Dungeness, and Skokomish. Available in most sporting goods stores and from Frank Amato Publications (800-541-9498) and www.amatobooks.com.

Lodging

You are never far from a campground on the peninsula, but the region also has more cushy (and expensive) accommodations.

Lake Quinault Lodge: An historic inn on the shores of Lake Quinault. Rooms and restaurant. Winter packages. 360-288-2900. www.visitlakequinault.com

Lake Crescent Lodge: In operation since 1916, the lodge has rooms and cabins, restaurant and boat rentals. 360-928-3211. http://foreverlodging.com

Kalaloch Lodge: Above the sandy beach, between the Hoh and Queets, the lodge has rooms, cabins, a restaurant and store. Located next to the ONP campground. 360-962-2271. www.visitkalaloch.com

Sol Duc Hot Springs: Located on the upper Sol Duc in Olympic National Park, Sol Duc has cabins and rooms, hot and cold pools, restaurant and store. Near ONP campground. 866-4SOLDUC. www.visitsolduc.com

Log Cabin Resort: This venerable Lake Crescent resort has rooms, cabins, chalets, RV sites, a restaurant, rental rowboats and canoes, and supplies. 360-928-3325. www.logcabinresort.net

The Lost Resort: On the shore of Lake Ozette, the resort offers campsites, camping cabins, deli, store and accommodations. 360-963-2899. www.lostresort.com

Three Rivers Resort: Near the confluence of the Sol Duc and Bogachiel, and a couple miles from Rialto Beach, Three Rivers has cabins, RV sites, a restaurant and supplies. 360-374-5300. www.forks-web.com

Olson's Resort: This Sekiu resort has motel rooms, cabins, boat ramp, moorage, and is a short run from productive Strait of Juan de Fuca salmon and bottomfishing areas. 360-963-2311. www.olsonsresort.com.

Information and Contacts

Olympic National Park: General information; fishing regulations; campgrounds; trail and road conditions. Information 360-565-3130. (Wilderness Information Center 360-565-3100); www.nps.gov/olym

Olympic National Forest: Campsites and cabins; trails and trail conditions; information on lakes and rivers. 360-956-2402. www.fs.fed.us/r6/Olympic

USGS River Gauges: Current river levels and flows on major Olympic Peninsula rivers. http://waterdata.usgs.gov/wa/nwis/current

Washington Department Fish and Wildlife: General information; regulations; harvest reports; 360-902-2200. www.wdfw.wa.gov

Further Reading

Fishing Technique and Tackle

Best of B.C. Lake Fishing, Karl Bruhn
Dry Line Steelhead, Bill McMillan
Fly-Fishing Coastal Cutthroat Trout, Les Johnson
Fly-Fishing for Pacific Salmon, Ferguson, Johnson, Trotter
Fly-Fishing for Pacific Salmon II, (completely rewritten) Johnson & Ferguson
Sea-Run, Les Johnson
Spey Flies and Dee Flies, John Shewey
Spey Flies: How to Tie Them, Bob Veverka
Steelhead Fly-fishing and Flies, Trey Combs
Steelhead Fly-fishing, Trey Combs
The Steelhead Trout, Trey Combs
Anything by Roderick Haig-Brown

Natural History

A Natural History Guide: Olympic National Park, Tim McNulty
Mountain in the Clouds, Bruce Brown

History

Exploring the Olympic Mountains, compiled by Carstein Lien
Across the Olympic Mountains: The Press Expedition, 1889-90, Robert L Wood
Men, Mules and Mountains: Lieutenant O'Neil's Olympic Expeditions, Robert L. Wood

Fish Science and Biology

Coastal Cutthroat Trout Diet in South Puget Sound, Washington 1999-2002, Joseph M. Jauquet
Extent of Anadromy in Bull Trout and Implications for Conservation of a Threatened Species, Samuel J. Brenkman and Stephen C. Corbett
Historic Steelhead Abundance in North Coast and Puget Sound Streams, Bill McMillan for the Wild Salmon Center
Pacific Salmon and Wildlife: Ecological Contexts, Relationships, and Implications for Management, C. Jeff Cederholm, et al
Shoreline Alteration in Hood Canal and the Eastern Strait of Juan de Fuca, Ron Hirschi, Ted Labbe, Alan Carter-Mortimer
Summary of Fisheries and Limnological Data for Lake Crescent, Washington, John Meyer and Steven Fradkin
Use of Otilith Chemistry and Radiotelemetry to Determine Age-Specific Migratory Patterns of Anadromous Bull Trout in the Hoh River, Washington, Samuel J. Brenkman, Stephen C. Corbett and Eric C. Vole

INDEX

E

F

G

H

I

P

Q

R

S

Photo Contributions

Dick Wentworth: 22, 24, 26, 27 32, 36, 96, 97, 98, 103

Doug Rose: 12, 44, 45, 48, 60, 61, 80, 88, 90, 104, 105, 119, 121, 125, 126

Eliana Rose: 46

Jeffery Delia: 77

Joe Uhlman: 6, 11, 14, 56, 58, 59, 67, 68, 70, 76, 87, 101, 107, 127, 128

John McMillan: 2, 4, 8, 10, 15, 16, 17, 18, 19, 20, 21, 28, 34, 86, 113, 114, 115, 116, 122, 123

Ron Hirschi: 50, 78

Photo Courtesy of Olympic National Park: 12, 13

Washington State Historical Society: 91